From the Book to the Book

EDMOND JABÈS

From the Book to the Book

An Edmond Jabès Reader

Translated from the French by
ROSMARIE WALDROP,
with additional translations by Pierre Joris,
Anthony Rudolf, and Keith Waldrop

WESLEYAN UNIVERSITY PRESS
Published by University Press of New England
Hanover and London

Wesleyan University Press
Published by University Press of New England, Hanover, NH 03755
This collection © 1991 by Wesleyan University;
"The Graven Silence of Writing" © 1991 by Richard Stamelman
All rights reserved
Printed in the United States of America 5 4 3 2 1
CIP data appear at the end of the book

"In Place of a Foreword" and "Cut of Time," © 1990 by Station Hill Press, from *From the Desert to the Book*, Station Hill Press, 1990, are used with permission of the publisher; "Songs for the Ogre's Feast" and "Seasons," © 1991 by Rosmarie Waldrop, are translated from *Je batis ma demeure*, © 1975 by Editions Gallimard; "Sunland" and "The Pact of Spring," © 1988 by Station Hill Press, from *If There Were Anywhere But Desert*, Station Hill Press, 1988, are used with permission of the publisher; "The Dispossessed Moment" and "The Stranger," © 1979 by Anthony Rudolf, from *A Share of Ink*, Menard Press, London, 1979, are used with permission of the publisher. Selections from *The Book of Questions*: The Book of Questions, © 1976 by Rosmarie Waldrop, translated from *Le livre des questions*, © 1963 by Editions Gallimard; *The Book of Yukel, Return to the Book*, © 1977 by Rosmarie Waldrop, translated from *Le livre de Yukel* and *Le retour au livre*, © 1964 and 1965 respectively by Editions Gallimard. *Yaël, Elya, Aely*, © 1983 by Rosmarie Waldrop, translated from *Yaël, Elya*, and *Aely*, © 1967, 1969, and 1972 respectively by Editions Gallimard. *El or the Last Book*, © 1984 by Rosmarie Waldrop, translated from *El, ou le dernier livre*, © 1973 by Editions Gallimard. Selections from *The Book of Resemblances*: The Book of Resemblances, © 1990 by Rosmarie Waldrop, translated from *Le livre des ressemblances*, © 1976 by Editions Gallimard. *Intimations The Desert*, © 1991 by Rosmarie Waldrop, translated from *Le soupçon le désert*, © 1978 by Editions Gallimard. *The Ineffaceable The Unperceived*, © 1991 by Rosmarie Waldrop, translated from *L'ineffaçable l'inaperçu*, © 1980 by Editions Gallimard. Selections from *The Little Book of Subversion Above Suspicion*, © 1991 by Rosmarie Waldrop, translated from *Le petit livre de subversion hors de soupçon*, © 1982 by Editions Gallimard. Selections from *The Book of Dialogue*, © 1987 by Rosmarie Waldrop, translated from *Le livre du dialogue*, © 1984 by Editions Gallimard. Selections from *The Journey*, © 1991 by Rosmarie Waldrop, translated from *Le parcours*, © 1985 by Editions Gallimard. "In Place of an Afterword," © 1991 by Rosmarie Waldrop, translated from *Dans la double dépendence du dit* and *Ça suit son cours*, Fata Morgana, © 1975, 1985 by Edmond Jabès.

Contents

The Graven Silence of Writing

> Words mark us as intensely as we mark them. Words for
> joy. Words for misfortune. Words for indifference and for
> hope. Words for things and for men. Words for the universe
> and words for nothingness.
>
> And behind each of them, life, in its simplicity or com-
> plexity, menaced by death.
>
> —*The Book of Margins*

Reading is physical, and it is violent. No matter how carefully we
pick up a book or how gently we open its cover, the binding cracks,
the pages cling to one another as if afraid to face the light, the cover
continually rises up to push away the hand holding it. From the first
page the book announces itself as a place of pain, suffering, and rupture. At the threshold of the book stands the devastating experience
of death and loss, as Edmond Jabès, one of France's most important
postwar writers and one of the most probing commentators in the
twentieth century of the mysteries of the Book, never ceases to assert
in over twenty works of aphoristic prose and poetry. From the first
words that blacken the white page, setting in motion a journey that
will have no end, a wandering that will know no rest, Jabès reveals
the exilic and destructive power of writing, the endless, discontin-
uous, fragmented, nomadic, always interrogative discourse that
forms and unforms, constructs and deconstructs, the book. "Mark
the first page of the book with a red marker," announces one of the
epigraphs to *The Book of Questions*. "For, in the beginning, the
wound is invisible." As the words of pain move across the white
pages like the footsteps of exiles on the desert sand, they offer tes-
timony to the loss of life, of family, of homeland, which characterizes
the history of Judaism. "There is nothing at the threshold of the open
page, it seems, but this wound of a race born of the book, whose
order and disorder are roads of suffering. Nothing but this pain,
whose past and whose permanence is [*sic*] also that of writing." The
story of the book is thus the story of "*wounds become writing*." Read-

ing is the "'becoming aware of a scream.'" The first word is always
a word of mourning, and "the point of any pen is that of a cry": the
cry of unanswerable questions; the scream of two lovers whose words
are scattered like ashes by the horrors of Auschwitz; the frightened
voices of men and women separated from an absent, silent, withdrawn God; the lamentations of exiled words searching endlessly to
recover a lost homeland. For Jabès, "'all the shadows in the world
are screams.'"

The Poetics of the Book

That the book should be the place of stifled screams, of silent
tears, of wounds that never heal "in a world torn with departures,"
that it should be the place of unending questions, of fragmented
speech, of uprooted quotations, of words in exile, and of a writing
forever circling back on itself, reveals the extent to which the book
is for Jabès the world. Since our perceptions of reality are essentially
linguistic, everything that exists in the world exists through language, everything that breathes or feels or cries does so in the book.
Not in one book, but in innumerable books, an unending sequence
of volumes generated by a writing that like a river never stops flowing. Sometimes this discourse is visible in the ink-black words on
the surface of the page, sometimes it courses invisibly through the
hidden parts of the text: in the white spaces between letters, in the
open expanses of margins, and behind the words themselves. The
page is not a flat surface; it has considerable depth. Within its sub-
textual labyrinth all kinds of hidden movements, transformations,
and subversions take place. What is behind or underneath the page
works to unsettle what is written on the surface; the wrinkles on the
face of the page are but shadows of what transpires beneath its features. Within the writing moves a counterwriting. Somewhere
among the entwined layers of the book lies an essential, invisible
book, the great unwritten—and ultimately unwriteable—Book that
every book vainly seeks to resemble and to rewrite. One book takes
up where another leaves off because the Book of Books, that mute,
invisible, unseizable work, that enigmatic and endlessly deferred
shadow book, that absent, messiah text of an absent God who has
withdrawn from the universe and from Creation, remains forever
unrevealed: "In back of the book there is the ground of the book. In

back of the ground there is immense space and, hidden in this immense space, the book we are going to write in its enigmatic sequence."

Writing is in exile, lost in a desert of whiteness, where it leaves traces of its endlessly circular wandering. The end of every book—in reality, more a beginning than an end—is always provisional, because only through the errancy of words does the book come to know the incompleteness of its textual existence and only through this homelessness to realize that the unrevealed and inexhaustible Book still remains to be written. "Any book is but a dim likeness of the lost book," Jabès writes. It is always with tentative hope that the words of a new book set out in search of the absent Book, a journey that will involve more wandering, more unanswered questions, more fragmented and incomplete writing, and therefore more failure. In writing over twenty books—from the seven volumes of *The Book of Questions* to the three volumes of *The Book of Resemblances*, from *The Book of Dialogue* and *The Book of Shares* to *The Book of Hospitality*, from *The Book of Margins* to *The Little Book of Subversion above Suspicion* and to *A Stranger with a Small Book Beneath His Arm*—Jabès has in a sense written only one book. And even that book, despite the thousands of pages and millions of words precariously gathered together to express the pain, loss, and suffering as well as the joy, friendship, and love of the Jewish—which is to say the human—condition, has been powerless to give voice to the inexpressible Book, which only death can write. For writing is where death transpires, where the "wondrous course of death" unfolds: "Writing . . . has that supreme power we grant above all to death, the power to transform the world, to justify the image of the universe in its many unknowable changes." In the beginning was not the word, but death. It is the pre-text that the word strives to translate and fashion into a text. Death in the form of the void, the nothing, the desert and as an experience of absence, lack, exile, effacement, erasure, and silence takes up residence in the text. The place of the book is a place of loss. To write, Jabès observes, "is to accept, or better yet, to seek a permanent confrontation with death." Never is writing a victory over nothingness; to the contrary, it is "an exploiting of nothingness through the word."

In the totality of Jabès's work there is a continual passage, an unending errancy from book to book, for, as he writes, "there is no end

to the sea or the book." As a writer and a reader—for Jabès the two
are coincident—he moves in a circle, or more precisely in a spiral,
from the book-to-be-written to the written book, the one that his
writing and reading have "accomplished." But in that illusory "completion" is the realization that the elusive Book still remains to be
created. The writer has no mastery over what he has written because
the book writes him as much as he writes it: "you are the one who
writes and who is written," announces the opening page of *The Book
of Questions*. The work he writes leads him endlessly toward a book
that remains to be discovered. Since the book is in a state of perpetual becoming and unending errancy, to which the painful incompleteness of every work bears witness, and since the very writing of
a book reveals the text that still remains unwritten, every new reading is also a *re*reading and every new book a *return* to the book. In
writing and reading the book, the writer and the reader always repeat it, for they are continually in movement *from* the book *to* the
book. The words of Yukel in *Return to the Book* could be applied to
Jabès as well: "I see ever farther, pushed by I do not know what
need to understand and love, farther yet till I shall find myself back
at my point of departure. What matter where I think I am going if
any course inevitably returns to our origins. We never overtake our
steps." There is no transcending the book, for "the beyond of the
book is still the book." Thus, the three volumes of *The Book of Resemblances*, coming in the wake of the seven volumes of *The Book
of Questions*, rewrite these books, or more particularly repeat in per-
petually different ways the trajectory of their themes, the swervings
of their endless questions, and the turnings of those "obsessional
words" that haunt Jabès's writing, words like "book," "God," "Jew,"
"vocable," "question," "desert," "threshold," and "stranger." *The
Book of Resemblances* takes us "to the other bank of the same inexhaustible book." It is a repetition of a book already written (and read)
and of texts yet to be written (and read), but the words, vocables,
questions, and fragments it repeats constitute an always different
writing. "The work I write immediately rewrites itself in the book,"
Jabès remarks. "This repeatability is part of its own breathing and of
the reduplication of each of its signs."

Jabès's endless questions, laconic aphorisms, and diasporic fragments give existence to a nomadic writing of indeterminacy and
doubt, a discourse that often walks in the traces of its own forgotten

steps. God's wandering word has for echo, Jabès remarks, "the word
of a wandering people. No oasis for it, no shadow, no peace. Only
the immense, thirsty desert, only the book of this thirst, the devastating fire of this fire reducing all books to ashes at the threshold
of the obsessive, illegible Book bequeathed us." The fate of the word
is the fate of the Jew, "because being Jewish means exiling yourself
in the word and, at the same time, weeping for your exile."

The Rupture of the Question

In Jabès's work the question is, as Didier Cahen has remarked,
"the 'passport' that allows one to move about in the land of the book."
It is the typography that explains the topography, the questing word
that uncovers the inscrutable world. More powerfully than answers,
which represent immobility, sedentariness, stability, closure, and
completion, the question in its essential nomadism can open doors,
point the way, reveal the path to follow. For it is an errant word,
expressive of exile, rupture, movement, and uncertainty. The question follows a quest not for an answer but for deeper and more dif-
ficult questions, although Jabès does acknowledge that " 'sometimes
a question is the flash of an answer.' " Yet, this ephemeral answer is
often just another question: " 'What will we get out of all the answers
which only lead to more questions, since questions are born of unsatisfactory answers?' asked the second disciple. / 'The promise of a
new question,' replied Reb Mendel." Questioning is a form of existence, a mode of being in the world. Through the question one
touches the mystery of a life, the reality of another person. *"Being
means questioning,"* Jabès remarks. *"Means interrogating yourself
in the labyrinths of the Question put to others and to God, and which
does not expect any answer."*

Questioning lies at the heart of the Jewish quest for identity, for
"the Jew answers every question with another question." Since the
condition of the Jew in the world is one of loss, separation, and exile—the effect of History and of God's absence, His mute withdrawal
from Creation out of which has arisen what Jabès calls a "Judaism
after God"—the question speaks the very language of lack; it is incomplete speech, a word longing for the missing words that could
give it the meaning it has lost or never possessed. If "rupture is at
the heart of my books" and "there is no language for unity, only

language for separation," as Jabès asserts, then the question alone among forms of speech can maintain the openness of the rupture, of the wound. There is no way to reach God except through the ineffaceable separation, the tear in the fabric of Creation, which His self-willed absence has produced. Only the questioning word can operate within this state of division and lack. The question circumscribes a void in which the writer, if he or she is truly a writer, must lead his or her life, accepting the sovereignty of the question and therefore the continual absence and postponement of an answer. Writing does not for Jabès offer mastery of the world. Despite thousands of words and the endless gathering of sentences, his books do not bestow knowledge, power, or possession: "'True knowledge is daily awareness that, in the end, one learns nothing. The Nothing is also knowledge, being the reverse of the All, as the air is the reverse of the wing.'"

Certainty is beyond Jabès's grasp even though one might assume the contrary from his tendency to give his aphoristic declarations the air of authority and terse finality one associates with definitions: "Knowledge means questioning," "The book is a labyrinth," "God is the blank present," "Every look contains the law," "*All writing is graven silence*," "*To read is to burn*." But the air of assurance and absolute certainty that surrounds these aphoristic declarations is false. Each assertion is contested and undone by the enigmatic reality of the subject it expresses: knowledge, the book, God, writing, reading. These aphoristic definitions are subverted from within by the implicit questions they raise about the nature of knowledge, the coherence of the book, the presence of God, the continuity of writing, and the protocols of reading. Jabès knows that no matter what answer one may put forward, it settles nothing; it raises more questions than it has answered. Continually, he tries out responses to an infinite number of unresolved and haunting questions that trail him from book to book: "Who is the Jew?" "What is a stranger?" "What is memory?" "Is dialogue possible?" "What is hospitality?" "To whom do I belong?" "Whom do I resemble?" And the aphorisms he invents, with their dense and enigmatic language and the sense of an essential completeness and totality distilled into a node of linguistic certainty, belie the incompleteness and indeterminacy that a language of enigma and paradox translate. These aphorisms are a nodal language composed of fragments; they leave the reader face to face with mystery; their contradictions raise a host of unanswerable questions: *"A voice wants a face / where we no longer see"*; *"You took your turn on the road of exile. / Ah, you were not alone. Therefore you walked alone"*; *"God is the measured and immeasurable death of God."* Here a language of aphoristic hermeticism cries out for interpretation, for a talmudic-like exegesis.

The Narrative of Exile

There is, of course, no shortage of characters well trained to offer such talmudic interpretations, especially in Jabès's early works. *The Book of Questions, The Book of Yukel, Return to the Book,* and *The Book of Resemblances* overflow with rabbinic voices and names from A (Reb Alcé, Reb Abbani, Reb Akri) to Z (Reb Zolé, Reb Zeilein, Reb Zalal). Even in the selections that have been brought together in the present collection there are over one hundred and twenty different names of rabbis—from Reb Nadir to Reb Mazaltov—all figments of Jabès's rich, talmudic imagination. What, one may wonder, is the function of these imaginary rabbis and the fictional quotations ascribed to them? Although each rabbi is no more or less than the words he is reported to have said—his existence defined and circumscribed by quotation—each is in his own brief textual appearance a character in the continuing story of exile and loss that book after book recounts. Through these rabbis Jabès is able to distance himself from his feelings, thoughts, doubts, and anguish in order to gain a better understanding of them and at the same time to probe the inner depths of his own being. Distance and intimacy coexist in this self-examination. The rabbis are *personae,* surrogates for his own being, as are most of the characters one encounters in Jabès's works: Sarah Schwall, Yukel Serafi, Nathan Seichell, Yaël, Elya, Aely, the man who meets a tailor who has survived the Holocaust ("Le Sud" in *The Book of Yukel,* not included here), and the writer visited in his study by a young woman with a strange question to ask, in "The Dream" (from *The Book of Dialogue*). Because "the 'I' is the miracle of the 'You,'" because the self depends on the stranger, who is always an other, because the "JE" (a reversal of the initials of Edmond Jabès's name) is also an "étrange-je" (an estranged and a strange "I")—for are we not strangers to ourselves, do we not, in the deepest reaches of our unconscious, harbor unrecognizable selves?

—Jabès cannot help but surrender to the *otherness* of writing, to its autonomous movement. He is indeed as much the one who is written as he is the one who writes. Through writing the "I" becomes the "you," JE becomes EJ, the self becomes the other.

Jabès's rabbis are singular and privileged interpreters of the Book; in other words, they are gifted readers. Their commentaries are designed to decipher the text, to reveal signs of the never-to-be-written Book in the words that are hidden behind the words. They search for the "white writing" which has been covered over by the dark words they read. For these rabbis, who are kabbalistic in spirit if not temperament, the change of a single letter can bring about a radical transformation in the universe. We cannot forget as well that these rabbis are also writers. Through their commentaries they create new works, because reading is, essentially, a creative act. As one reads, as one interprets, one also writes. Reading is not the passive search for an anterior meaning that has been hidden in a text like buried treasure, but rather the activating of an errant language. Through reading, writing comes alive, is put in motion. Reading makes the text legible. One experiences the book as space and as movement rather than as meaning. The broken, fragmented, swerving, errant, and interrogative character of Jabès's writing calls into question the building up of meaning, the accumulation of knowledge, and the construction of sense, as readers have come to expect them from texts. The experience of Jabès's books is not one of possession but of dispossession. Reading is a form of exile, of wandering (with all the circuitous ambulations, detours, and dead ends that suggests) through a space without borders or margins, without geographical or narrative contours, and without fixed landmarks or visible ends. The desert is indeed, as Jabès repeatedly affirms, the true place of the word, its vast and silent domain: "Everywhere: oblivion, the unmade bed of absence, the wandering kingdom of dust. . . . When there is nothing left, there will still be sand. There will still be the desert to conjugate the nothing."

Despite the characters one finds in Jabès's books—the rabbis who utter their hermetic, gnomic riddles before quickly disappearing; the lovers, Sarah and Yukel, each consumed in a different way by the Holocaust; Yaël, mother of a stillborn child, who carries the double name of God (*Yahweh* and *El*) and whose murder by her lover allegorically dramatizes God's homicidal and suicidal killing of His

Creation; Elya, the child born into death, who carries the reversed syllables of his mother's name and who is the "natural son of Nothing," the embodiment of an absence appropriated and given posthumous "life" in the after-death of a book; Aely, incarnation of a glance, a look, which is subservient to the law of the book, inhabitant of *"the elsewhere of an unimaginable elsewhere,"* who is the very essence of absence, of what has not yet been thought, of the apocalyptic void that "branches out beyond existence. Beyond you, Yaël. In Elya's wake"; and finally, El, the name of God, who in withdrawing from the world leaves the trace of a small dot, symbol for the effacement of the book reduced to a tiny mark by words that in continually writing themselves over write over themselves—there is very little *sense* of character in Jabès's books. Even though he projects his life and thought into his personages, they lack physicality. Rarely are they described; rarely are we told what they look like; rarely do we know where they live. Jabès seems reluctant to represent them, to give them figuration, as if he wished to obey the Second Commandment's interdiction against graven images. But flesh and blood characters are not what he is after; it is not bodies that interest him but words. His characters are, above all, the vocables and the silences they speak. They may be disembodied, but they are not speechless. The body of language, the corporeality of writing, puts flesh on their bones. They gain presence—even though most of them are incarnations of absence (Yaël is murdered, Elya stillborn, Aely lost at the outer reaches of death's void, El withdrawn into a dot)—through the writing they embody.

Jabès's characters are spokespersons; they carry his words and are carried away by them. And yet, not much narrative reality surrounds them. The histories and stories of their lives are given only in the broadest of terms (with perhaps the exception of Sarah and Yukel, who are the most developed personages in all the books) and often without precise temporal or spatial indications. As characters who only appear *en passant,* who surface at different and unexpected moments of the writing, and who receive neither uninterrupted description nor continuous development, they take on the errancy and impersonality of the writing itself. The movement of their lives comes from the turnings and hesitations of the book. Such indeterminacy of character is echoed by an indeterminacy of narrative. Jabès eschews conventional narrative logic, preferring instead a breathless, interrupted style, full of breaks, deferrals, postponements, and silences. The story of Sarah and Yukel, more hinted at than told, is expressed, for example, in bits and pieces over the course of three books. The characters appear at irregular intervals, referring obliquely to their experiences in laconic meditations and aphoristic reflections. Sarah and Yukel move in and out of the book's shadows, its questions, quotations, and rabbinic voices, more absent than present, sometimes in the foreground, sometimes hidden in the wings, their lamentations lost in the roar of other forms of flowing and cascading writing. They, like the other characters, are marked by the anonymous reality of writing, of a textual space not unlike the desert or the sea, where it is easy to lose one's way and where the conventional dimensions of time and space no longer have meaning.

It may be that the "stories" of Jabès's characters and of Sarah and Yukel in particular must remain laconic and abbreviated, for theirs is the account "of a love destroyed by men and by words. It has the dimension of the book and the bitter stubbornness of a wandering question." The horror of the history that crushes the two lovers renders any story, any retelling, meaningless. Only a writing of hesitancy, discontinuity, and fragmentariness can evoke the terrifying end of time and history announced by the Shoah. The catastrophe of Auschwitz makes narration all but impossible and, while calling into question the nature of representation in general, demands a radically different kind of writing.

This may explain perhaps why Jabès's works are "books" and not "novels." The novel, he explains to Marcel Cohen in their interview published in *From the Desert to the Book* (Barrytown, N.Y.: Station Hill Press, 1990), is the very opposite of the book. While the novelist exercises control over the writing, while he or she turns the space of the text into the space of the story to be retold, the writer of the book allows the writing to dominate. The book "recounts" or, more precisely, activates not a story but the movement of writing. The novelist masters his or her writing in order to put it at the service of the characters. By imposing on the novel a word that is manifestly exterior to the writing, the novelist assassinates the book. Ignorant of the rhythm and respiration punctuating the book's circular and enigmatic writing, the novelist is word-deaf. He or she does not know, as does the writer of the book, how to listen to the page and to the reverberations of its whiteness and silence. The true writer, who is not a creator but a listener, is sensitive to the book's orality, to its freedom as uninterrupted language, to the void and silence that hide within it, to its rejection of closure, and, above all, to the invisible, forgotten, absent, always virtual book it shelters. It is the aleatory movement of writing, its swerving away from a predetermined destination and a perceived end, that endows the Jabèsian book with its singular freedom and the Jabèsian narrative with its unique rejection of closure: "'You are a storyteller,' a friend said to me one day. / How can I be when words and images always cut in and want to be heard with their own aura, when the story is built out of bits of counter-stories, and when silence lies in wait for the world?"

The Diaspora of Words

"Immense is the hospitality of the book," Jabès writes in *The Book of Hospitality* (1991), published a few months after his death. There is hardly a written form, a pattern of speech, a linguistic phenomenon, and a literary genre that is not welcomed into the world of the book. Questions, quotations, dialogues, meditations, aphorisms, commandments, fragments, prayers, cries, hymns, songs, poems, fables, stories, journal entries, commentaries, letters to friends, nursery rhymes, notes, threnodies, incantations—the catalogue is limitless—flow through the pages of the book. One is overwhelmed by the multiplicity of voices, by the rich and varied audibility of words, by assonances, rhymes, refrains, echoes, resonances, silences, and *jeux de mots*. The magnetic field of the text attracts puns and word games of all kinds. Change the configuration of letters in a word and one succeeds in changing the order of the universe. So *Yaël* becomes *Elya* who becomes *Aely* who in turn becomes *El*, the name of God, whose letters, reversed, frame the word "*livre*." Or the words "écrit" ("the written") and "récit" ("the tale") form "*one and the same word with its letters scrambled in a most natural way.*" Jabès reveals the words that lie hidden in other words: *ou* ("or") in *pour* ("for"); *autour* ("around") in *vautour* ("vulture"); *mur* ("wall") in *amour* ("love"); *erre* ("wander") in *terre* ("earth"); *nul* ("nothing") in *l'un* ("the one"); *Dieu* ("God") in *deuil* ("mourning"). This linguistic heterocosm is matched by a plethora of typographic forms and signs: roman and italic print in different point sizes, inverted commas, dashes, question marks, parentheses, indentations, paragraphs occupying different positions on a page, and white spaces not only at the margins but dispersed over the surface of the page. Writing becomes dissemination, its movement that of diaspora. The page is the place where absences are written. Everywhere in Jabès's books there is a self-referential awareness of writing as act, as movement, as dispersion, as flow. The titles of different chapters, for example, self-consciously refer to their own status as text, as book, as scriptural reality: "Forespeech," "At the Threshold of the Book," "And You Shall Be in the Book," "The Book of the Absent," "Dialogue of Stone and Sand," "The Story," "Pre-Dialogue," "The Book Belongs Only to the Book," "The Book Read, Here Begins the Reading of the Book."

The linguistic form, however, most unique to Jabès's books and most mysterious in its workings is the *vocable*. A term used for centuries primarily by linguists, it has been taken up by Jabès and given new meaning. For the vocable is not merely a word; it is the spoken word as it exists in the interior of the book. It is the word as it "speaks" within the silence of the book. The vocable is not only read, it is also heard. It has an orality that is fused to its legibility, a visibility that participates in its audibility. Both eye and ear must read it. Enveloped by silence, it still can be seen; masked by invisibility, it still can be heard. Enigma that it is, the vocable is fundamentally subversive, separating itself from the language environment it inhabits in order to find within the depths of language the other writing, the white writing, which every text hides as the sea hides the sand. The vocable is "the word, which shatters the word in order to break free, [and which] for a moment holds the key to the book."

With waves of writing, cascades of words, vocables, signs, voices, and typographic forms coursing through the pages of so many books, and with meaning often suspended or deferred, reading Jabès can be a challenging, if not a daunting, experience. It is Jabès's intention to make the reader wander, to make him or her participate in the nomadism of the text. Reading is a form of errancy, and the book is a place of passage: *"you must tackle my work in its circles. / And each of them will demand a new reading,"* he advises. The Jabèsian book is, as he has observed, like an empty envelope. One expects a message, but none is found because the sender forgot to enclose the letter. The reader must remember that it is the encounter with writing, with its meanderings, swerves, detours, and errant motions, that counts above all in Jabès's works. Meaning, certainty, and knowledge are incompatible with writing. For this reason, writing is an act of subversion that seeks to deconstruct any kind of *savoir magistral*, any kind of systematized or imperial knowledge. Yet, Jabès's books are not unreadable or obscure, as he is quick to assert. They only become unreadable when one is looking for certainty. Their readability is dependent on the deferral of meaning. As long as the reader yields to the fluency and the flow of writing and to the accumulation of fragments, which mutate and multiply endlessly, as long as he or she understands how one book unwrites an earlier book by rewriting it, as long as he or she does not stop at every sentence to try to find some meaning behind the paradox, some logic behind the contradiction, then the experience of the Jabèsian text as exile, as wandering, as diaspora, and as enigma will be enhanced.

The Book of Life

Edmond Jabès, at every moment of his life, was ahead of his time. Born in Cairo on April 16, 1912, to an upper-middle-class Jewish family of Italian nationality, he was mistakenly declared born two days earlier. What would seem an inconsequential error on a birth certificate was for Jabès of major significance. His identity as a person, as a writer, and as a Jew was affected. Suddenly, he was no longer a single, undivided self, but a man invaded by an other who shared his name and existence. There spoke from within him another voice, another poem, another book. "The two days added to my life could only be lived in death," he writes in *Elya*. "As is true for the book, as is true for God in the world, the first manifestation of my existence was that of an absence that carried my name." The realities of lack, absence, and otherness, which were to become the major themes of his work, appear to have been graven from birth into Jabès's being. The dialogue with the other so beautifully expressed in *The Book of Dialogue* (1984), the love for the stranger, incarnation of the difference that endows every human being with a radiant singularity, which *A Stranger with a Small Book Beneath His Arm* (1989) movingly examines, the desire for sharing and love, which *The Book of Shares* (1987) presents, and the essential importance of hospitality, which is a form of dialogue and sharing offered to the other, to the stranger in his or her radical difference, as *The Book of Hos-*

pitality (1991) so humanly reveals, point to a preoccupation with otherness and with the absence or distance of the other (whether a loved one, a stranger, God, the Jew, the book) that characterizes most of Jabès's writing, especially the works written during the last ten years of his life. Naming the other, welcoming the stranger, responding to and taking responsibility for the unknown person who suddenly appears from nowhere are concerns that originate perhaps from Jabès's inaccurate birth certificate.

Although intellectually marked as he seemed to have been by the reality of his mistaken birthdate, Jabès in early adolescence was devastated emotionally by an event of surpassing gravity and sorrow, the death of his sister from tuberculosis at the age of twenty-two. Jabès, who was twelve at the time, was alone with his sister when she died and for the first time in his life understood, as he told Marcel Cohen, that death had a language of its own radically different from that of life. The words of the dying are already touched by a distance and an otherness that the language of the living cannot express. The unforgettable voice of his dying sister, in its serenity and distance, its tone of fatalistic resignation and its awareness of impending separation, reverberates throughout *The Book of Questions*. The memory of her death is memorialized in the torn words, the distant speech, and the absent meanings of all of Jabès's writing.

Yet, Jabès's life in Egypt before World War II was, generally speaking, tranquil. He attended French schools, met and married his wife, Arlette Cohen, raised two daughters, and continued to write poetry influenced by such French surrealist writers and friends as Max Jacob, Paul Eluard, and René Char. But in 1942, with the Germans advancing, Jabès was evacuated by the British to Palestine, where he lived for nine months until it was safe to return to Egypt. After the war more collections of his poetry were published, and he worked actively as a contributor to several French literary reviews in Cairo and Paris. In 1957, in the wake of the Suez crisis, Jabès was forced, as were all Jews and Egyptians of Jewish descent, to leave Egypt. He never returned. Settling in Paris with little money and a family to support, he took a job with an advertising company, finding time to write only at night, on weekends, and while commuting on the *métro*. It is from 1957, and his exile in France, that Jabès began to write in a different way. The richly metaphorical, sometimes surrealistic, poetry of the Egyptian years gave way to the fragmented, dense, and sparse prose of *The Book of Questions*. The poem yielded to the book, although Jabès in his prose never ceased to write as a poet. And strangest of all, the desert, so powerfully present in Jabès's daily life in Cairo, appeared for the first time as a major theme of his writing.

Between 1957 and his death on January 2, 1991, Jabès continued to write his extraordinary sequence of books, to publish collections of poetry, and to raise his voice in essays of different kinds against the rise of racism and anti-Semitism throughout the world. Translated into Italian, Spanish, German, Swedish, Hebrew, Japanese, and English, Jabès's works are widely credited for having renewed interest in the poetics and the poetry of the book. Not since Mallarmé in the latter half of the nineteenth century has a poet—and Jabès is indeed a poet of both prose and verse—been so possessed by the expressive power of the book, by the poetry of the blank page, and by the visibility and invisibility of writing. Not since the rabbis, the talmudists, and the kabbalists of the past has a writer so passionately emphasized the magical power of letters to rewrite the world. And not since the time when nomads wandered the earth has a man so eloquently experienced the desert which lies at the bottom of every word and which designates the nothingness and the void that in our age have become the indelible legacies of Auschwitz: the splintering word within every word and the piercing cry that is the unhealable wound of language.

Richard Stamelman

Note: Readers interested in learning more about Edmond Jabès's work may wish to consult the following studies: Didier Cahen, *Edmond Jabès* (Paris: Belfond, 1991); Eric Gould, ed., *The Sin of the Book: Edmond Jabès* (Lincoln: University of Nebraska Press, 1985); Warren F. Motte, Jr., *Questioning Edmond Jabès* (Lincoln: University of Nebraska Press, 1990); and Richard Stamelman, *Lost Beyond Telling: Representations of Death and Absence in Modern French Poetry* (Ithaca: Cornell University Press, 1990).

When Silence Speaks

The texts that Edmond Jabès has assembled here span seventeen books and the years between 1943 and 1985. They form a carefully composed journey through his work, in which his themes appear in a new orchestration, a different juxtaposition of voices. It allows the reader to follow, in time-lapse, the author's own life-journey from one book to the next, always pushing beyond categories and limits, always in confrontation with The Book, the absent, nonexistent Book, which is not only the empty center of Jabès's work, but also the ground of all books, as the unthought is the ground of all thinking.

All of Jabès's books explore the double wound of consciousness, our being set apart from the rest of creation in the glorious and murderous species of humankind, and set apart from our fellow humans as individuals, again always *other*. Let us not forget, said Jabès in a recent article, that "if we say 'I' we already say *difference*." His work explores the nature of book and word, of man defining himself through the word against all that challenges him: death, silence, the void, the infinite—or God, our symbol for all these.

Jabès's image of God is that of Judaism, and the theme of otherness is focused in the figure of the Jew, a challenge to our craving for unity (which is at the basis of intolerance), even beyond persecution and holocaust. This is less because Edmond Jabès was Jewish and steeped in the talmudic tradition than because Judaism is exemplary of the human condition: it offers both a (paradoxically) collective experience of singularity and a culture explicitly defined by a book, the Bible. "I have spoken of the difficulty of being Jewish, which is the same as the difficulty of writing," he said in *The Book of Questions*, "because Judaism and writing are one and the same waiting, one and the same hope, and one and the same wearing down."

From the Book to the Book might seem radically different from Jabès's other books in that it has his tangible and significant oeuvre behind it rather than a missing core, like the untold story of *The Book of Questions,* or the nonexistent Book. But it also points to this empty center, though at one remove: pointing to books that point to the absent Book. This indirection also parallels or, rather, varies the structural indirection of the original books (after *I Build My Dwelling*) with their multiple, gradual approaches to "the book" through ground after ground, gateway after gateway, threshold after threshold, door after door. With the chapter actually called "The Book" usually the shortest, a kind of punctuation still pointing beyond.

Just as the nonexistence of God, the emptiness of transcendence, keeps Jabès's questions spiraling without ever homing in on an answer, so the absent Book is the pre-text that engenders the rabbinical commentaries, the reflections that oscillate between poetry and aphorism, the open, "exploded," nonlinear form of Jabès's work. For Jabès challenges the unifying tendency of our thinking not only through the theme of man's singularity, but also by breaking the discourse into fragments (repeating, as it were, the breaking of the Tablets of the Law: "The book is an unbearable totality. I write on facetted ground"), by opening language to silence, which calls the word into question, but also lets it breathe a larger air. Jabès's commentary, *commentaire,* teaches us how to be silent: *comment taire.*

The experience of silence, like that of the desert (crucial for Jabès), is one of listening. Jabès's writing does not "master" language, but listens to it, listens to language thinking and breathing, to words hidden within words that finally ambush the book and begin to play (often to the translator's despair!). It is a listening that encourages any statement to go farther, beyond its limits, beyond itself, and "only later encircles its vertiginous unfolding." Or, in John Ashbery's words, it "tricks the idea into being, then dismantles it," before it can freeze into doctrine.

Shifting voices and breaks of mode, tautologies, a-logical sequences and metaphors, a stress on uncertainty (the constant "perhaps" and conditional)—all combine to subvert the authority of statement, of closure and linearity, the confidence in a narrative thread, a continuity of temporal and causal sequence.

. Again, by fragmenting further an already fragmented work, *From the Book to the Book* raises discontinuity and openness to the second power. It is a mosaic of a mosaic, where silence speaks in the cracks, where, as Maurice Blanchot said, "the void becomes an achievement . . . and perhaps thought shows through."

Rosmarie Waldrop

From the Book to the Book

. . . as if all the truth carried in the book—this portion of dark where the light wears thin—were but an approach to death, for which writing is both chance and misfortune; a death becomes ours through every word, every letter, through sounds and silence, where sense is only what makes sense of the adventure. As if, moreover, in order to make sense, this adventure needed the deep sense of words, their multiple meanings, which are but focal points of their radiance.

Thus the book, carried by its words, lives through their intimate life and dies of sharing their death.

Thus we are first led on and then abandoned by every fraction of a second of our life. So that we can finally bear witness only to this abandonment.

In Place of a Foreword

A good reader is, first of all, a sensitive, curious, demanding reader. In reading, he follows his intuition.

Intuition—or what could pass as such—lies, for example, in his unconscious refusal to enter any house directly through the main door, the one that by its dimensions, characteristics and location, offers itself proudly as the main entrance, the one designated and recognized both outside and inside as the sole threshold.

To take the wrong door means indeed to go against the order that presided over the plan of the house, over the layout of the rooms, over the beauty and rationality of the whole. But what discoveries are made possible for the visitor! The new path permits him to see what no other than himself could have perceived from that angle. All the more so because I am not sure that one can enter a written work without having forced one's own way in first.

One needs to have wandered a lot, to have taken many paths, to realize, when all is said and done, that at no moment one has left one's own.

A door towards which we would have bent our steps, moved by I don't know what lost reason, what insatiable desire to unlearn or to founder in the abyss, will never have misled us, will never mislead us.

This is so doubtless because, in the book, there are no visible doors, and by evoking its order, its law, I allude only to the luminous progress from page to page by author and reader, both united in the same adventure and henceforth accountable only for their own steps.

To forget in order to know; to know in order to fill up the forgotten, in its own time.

The outcome belongs to nobody. The approach, however, depends entirely on us.

And if this house was in ruins? And if these ruins were the desert? It is the broken stone, it is every grain of sand that would then answer for our passage.

Translated by Pierre Joris

I Build My Dwelling

(1943–1957)

SONGS FOR THE OGRE'S FEAST
(1943–1945)

To the memory of Max Jacob

... because there is perhaps a song rooted deep in our child-hood, which, in the most murderous hour, can all by itself defy misery and death.

UNTITLED SONG

Ever since this story
birds have had four wings
brides a ring
tides a bouquet
rocks a tongue
to chatter to chatter . . .

Ever since this night
walls have had four roofs
sorrows a suit
beauty a nest
and beds a mast
to sail, to sail . . .

Ever since this wreck
the sea has had four arms
farewell all the rats
the pearl a dagger
the sky a kerchief
to cry in, to cry in . . .

SONG OF THE STRANGER

I'm looking for
a man I don't know,
who's never been more myself
than since I started to look for him.
Does he have my eyes, my hands
and all those thoughts like
flotsam of time?
Season of a thousand wrecks,
the sea no longer a sea,
but an icy watery grave.
Yet farther on, who knows how it goes on?
A little girl sings backward
and nightly reigns over trees
a shepherdess among her sheep.
Let us wrench thirst from the grain
of salt no drink can quench.
Along with the stones, a whole world eats
its heart out, being
from nowhere, like me.

SONG FOR TWO LAUGHS

A laugh in the water. You know what it does? Makes the water laugh.
It washes very carefully so it can humiliate the miserable laughs that
have neither water nor soap, only lice in their hair. The laugh is all
white. You might say a tame crab. It moves its head—which I think
means "Hello." It waves its hand—which I think means "Good-
bye." It tries to close my eyes because it is modest. Don't count on
me to anger this laugh. It already almost drowned once before.

LITTLE SONG
FOR A FAMILIAR IMAGE OF A LAZYBONES

The lazybones attracts all the waves of the sea. "Let me sleep," he
begs, "so nice and warm under my white sheets and blue blankets."
And would you believe it? The sun's on his side.

SONG
FOR THREE ASTONISHED DEAD MEN

Three dead men we were
didn't know why we'd come here
to this open grave.
The oldest said: "This is beautiful!"
The second: "It is hot . . ."
And I just barely awakened
what could I say but:
"Already?"
Three shadows we were
without lips or necks
laughs tucked
under our arms
for lack of dreams.
And a young girl
restored to the night
to keep us company.

Translated by Rosmarie Waldrop

SUNLAND

A country where the billboards have claws
Not just anyone can enter
Where the stones are outside earth's ravaged eyelids
Shadows there take a chance on
morning How many knots of thirst for fruit immobilize the branches
from the roots up
A country a town at the foot of a wall
where children play at catching the wind
at blinding the big blue eyes of the wind
where girls hike up their schnappsy dresses
at midnight
My love a country a town a room
prolonged by the oil of casements
cut short by the quartz of evening setting in
where the bolts are lock-boxes with dream keys
on which you write your name
where water runs between the fingers
when the lamp begins to flicker
My love a country a town a room a bed
The universe sprouts there in spider fronds lynx-pads
We hear life inflating the veins
of silence
All things take measure of themselves and rejoice
in their own form
My love a country a town a room a bed a dead man
which opens out
when nothing sounds
I never spoke to you about him
my brother my ally
the only one who remembers
who tells indefinitely the frozen beads of his soul
Pain sets fire
to shadows His temples become irridescent

unawares
My love a country a town a room a bed a dead man a roof
Cinderella rouses festive rings on the river
with her naked foot
The orchestra makes gold orgy-beans glitter
on heads of grizzled hair
We kill the same way we sing
A girl has lost her train of don't-care berries
and the lark of her anxieties
The mirrored seasons
throw down their marked cards
My love a country a town a room a bed a dead man
a roof a necklace
The fault is not with the fish-bone veil that we flay
nor with the pearl seeking refuge in the attic
The sailor has no trouble rhyming
His girl displays shark's-fin buckles
and a layered belt of fawn
My love a country a town a room a bed a dead man
a roof
I have returned the necklace
My love a country a town a room a bed a dead man
The roof has fallen in
My love a country a town a room a bed
The dead man is buried
My love a country a town a room
The bed is unmade
My love a country a town
The room is empty
My love a country
What town was it
My love our love
without a country

Translated by Keith Waldrop

SEASONS

The earth has burned its old saws
under the winter snow
Summer a translucent eggshell
Summer for vultures' mysterious flight

Woman with powdery wings
flat cyanide chest

Summer a mane of will-o'-the-wisps
held high on a breathtaking neck

The joy of trees admits of changing leaves
The monster with the riddle at her feet

Summer a lightweight key on the Lord Mayor's belly
Key of buried cities of cities to come
So many doors for a single key

Time has burned its cities
its villages its graying trees
Fall makes the bushes shed tears
as well as their parents' ghosts

Time has burned its fingers
at death's tempestuous touch

All windows are empty
A hen pecks for grain in her sleep
Dreams break the boredom of roads

The sky has drowned its twentieth-birthday scrapbook
Fear makes the soul blush in the cracks

Slashes are wrinkles Pain is avenged
Lips lack the courage to move

Elegant time is all dressed up
in gaiters and gloves
to confide in the dumb
and the blind

The stone offers its lovers
the same portrait at every age
the octopus its happy experience of wrecks

How many fish good
catch
can wriggle in one sound
New-come words discover the sea
The infinite speaks Its words scorch

Man with his eternal scissors
cuts a shadow his size from the light
his double a gentle giant with eyes of dust
a thumb of ivy an impatient bed

Tomorrow is an uncapped province
without greenery without scent
a well betrayed by its water

The steps of thirst are hollow with hope

I have walked with the random sound
that silence makes in the grass in the air
I have walked with the wind the old
vertigo of vaults The traveler's
final halt There is blood in the flowers
Vampires are haunting the parks

Tomorrow is a desert without chosen people
A farewell hatching its grapes

Wine in vain grows wing
after wing Tomorrow shunts off
every milestone's eye

Winter has burned its brandy
in the very first bar

Spring matches colors
to the slope of the copper claim

We have lost our house
by escaping from hours

Tomorrow's a beach glimpsed
at every turn of the stairs
desperate hair
in the lazy void of a dream
Tomorrow's for you whom I await
in memory's towering waves
in the haughty
suicide of breasts

Milk wallows in the ocean
an ermine in its pelt

Stars
bouquets of pride
in your hands

You are the will-o'-the-wisp youth of fire
the girdle's abyss of distress

Stems have pushed through the green veil solitude
The crown is missing from the savior's bent head

Translated by Rosmarie Waldrop

THE DISPOSSESSED MOMENT

The degeneration
　　of the moment
　　　　cut off
　　from its proud descendants
　　　　cut off
　　from its ancestors
　　　　　　black and white

with its scars revealed

　　Gold has the gift
　　　　of imitation
　　is hungry
　　　　for the bad days

At your doorstep you will know
the moment we have left to live

Translated by Anthony Rudolf

THE STRANGER

The coquetry of things
in seeming what they are
The world is a cotery
It's hard for the stranger
to make himself heard
He's reproached for his language
He's reproached for his gestures
And for his patient courtesy
reaps insults and threats

Translated by Anthony Rudolf

THE PACT OF SPRING

Words have worked their
way into mineshafts but have
lost my voice Silence capsized
inkwell The pen is the derelict
My two suns full-formed rivers
The sea is above the trees
Memory of leaves the hours
fête their flowers Sleep is
transparent fruit Night is
culled from the branches Tomorrow
has no shadow Our legend is
secret So wastes away
the dawn when canceled words
speak to those who never spoke
elect nothingness a bloodstain
Crumpled page pallid hand
clenched Leavetaking is limitless
The universe lives off oblivion stages
of stars Man and nature
share in kind and in kin
Thirst is of the earth Soft sheltering
flesh the very stones are
dreams To a hundred other evidences
the crystalline support of springs stolen
faces We no longer know where
we are to where we radiate
Youth of flintstones the beach
is the shingly port of the desert
the sandy witness of your
kingdoms haunted by reptiles
and widowed hawks The flight of
time affects a schoolboy wing
the colors the gold cycle it

pursues In the beak that pecks out eyes
is eternity in the venom
of roots chopped from the trunk
My groan is that of a wound
my song the die of desire
Stale water is absentee lord the other
tyrant whose form is the cold
Sulfur is seasonal the simple
gesture harbinger of ashes
Fire sprouting just beside
our doors our fields arranged
so that pain pulls in the
same yoke with hope
Dispossessed hands are
hands that mould us once the
defeat is told Lived cities
enslaved walls I run with the
sound of my running which rings with
a borrowed name I've no earth
but the earth Hence the day
finds no aperture For trump I've
only the luck of firm flagstones
to plant my feet on
A fate frolics with its
breathing and the oath
of its bondsmen the disbanded heavens
Noon with mirage of oars
in the ploughed air Shores have
their aviaries prisons of glass
At each cry the day flies
into pieces Winter's menace increases
a bitter rustling of our weapons
which the restless woman notes
The child carries the power of
living on his shoulders The
descent is in the loins Down there
is my love stricken eagle
Peaks are pedestals The
lips deliver up the key There

speech is a fateful deep
abyss Lamentation is the word's
bed river of confused voices
my two suns captive mirrors

Snow fastens its hair
to the flagpole of approaching dusk
The head is last to darken
along with the rainbow and the open
book Insignia of vain
victories a target offered
to echoes The palm goes to the prey
To the written the springtime the pact

Translated by Keith Waldrop

Cut of Time

I would say first of all that duration is evidently only a thing of the mind. What persists is what we stop at. It is a moment we do not manage to classify, whose consequences we do not manage to exhaust and whose effects we do not manage to neutralize.

Does that mean that we are right to persist so relentlessly? Did that moment really have the importance it takes on in our eyes? Or isn't it rather that we feed it with a sensibility, a culture, a nostalgia, in short, a *matter* that inflects it?

Both seem true to me. The point is that reality does not suffice for us. We cannot even seriously envisage it. It passes through something ineffaceable, something unnoticed that always keeps it at a distance.

For example, when we are in the grip of a strong emotion, we give it duration, that is to say we privilege it to the point of refusing the events that preceded or that will follow it and which alone could assign it its correct place. The most durable memories thus bear witness to an intellectual and nearly physical tensing. In its passage through thought, through words, every memory appears like a sickness of language. A psychiatrist, Adolfo Fernandez-Zoïla, shows this clearly in his treatise on trauma.

Does this suggest that we falsify events? Can we be certain about this? I, for one, don't think so; to the contrary: we refuse to lock the event into the instant. In fact, it is no longer the event that is at work on us, but its imprint, its trace, its sign. That's why every writer could say: To live means to write one's life.

Something else needs to be considered: we can live only in the event's reverberation. We cannot live in a frozen moment—we would be dead.

As I started to write *The Book of Questions*, I got the impression that the culture I had relied on so far was violently cracking up. At any rate, I felt that it was no longer able to channel the anxieties I was harboring. I no longer belonged—and foresaw that I would have to ground my writing in this not-belonging. Ragged phrases, shards of dialogue slowly surfaced—but as if from an anterior memory. Without knowing it, I was listening to a book rejecting all books and which I obviously did not master. I was interrogating this book even as I was writing it, expecting that it would create itself through the interrogation itself. But was it one book or were there innumerable books inside the book, from which its form, its ruptures come? In a way I had to track the book beyond its ruptures, to where it has no longer any belonging or place or resemblance, where therefore it escapes all categories and traditions.

Hence the excessive, nearly obsessional attention Jewish exegetes bring to the word, indeed to the letter—words they take to be the keepers of an even greater truth, despite the fact that most of the time they cannot formulate them.

My rabbis may be false rabbis but they are closer to me than any other decipherer, because they themselves are writers; they are, simultaneously, creators of and commentators on their own works. Isn't every true reader a potential writer, a "rabbi" rooted in the book?

You seem to detect a contradiction between the terms "memory" and "imagination." I don't see a contradiction here. To imagine— that can mean to recover, to re-create, what one has forgotten. My rabbis are thus simultaneously imaginary and drawn from the deepest layers of my memory—a memory I'm supposed to have lost every trace of, though this doesn't keep it from being just as piercingly painful, like something skinned alive.

As far as the story of Sarah and Yukel is concerned, there was no need to tell it. That's why it remains so fragmentary. Their personal biography is so crushed by the scope of the historical drama—the murder of six million men, women and children—that it cannot reflect it at all. That's exactly why their story is given only in small fragments. One needs only a few markers to recognize a path.

Sarah and Yukel talk as if they were already history's designated witnesses and victims, a history of which they would have been truly conscious only during brief moments of extreme lucidity.

·

"What more—or what less—could I say than what one can read in my books?

No doubt nothing that would resemble a closure, nothing that would lock them in on themselves, noth-

ing that would persist in abolishing the desert that
keeps them at the distance of what one would try to
make them say—and which, maybe, they do say, but
differently, with their own voice; for the desert is infinite; for their voice is older than mine and, inside my
limits, I could at best manage to adjust my voice piti-
fully to the undatable echoes of theirs."

.

Why render that experience through fiction? First, because we
are only fiction. We are only the idea we have of ourselves.

Fiction also permitted me to introduce the historical Jewish dimension and its drama into my books. I escaped the genocide. I
consider myself a survivor, not only as a Jew but simply as a man.

.

For a writer, to call himself into question means to
shield his book from any attempt at appropriation by
the reader, by depriving the latter of the possibility of
undertaking a global reading of the work. Unless one
could convince the reader—but this seems unthinkable to me—to modify his approach each time.

It is upon this unthinkable that *The Book of Questions* and *The Book of Resemblances* open.

To read them would thus mean to espouse each of
their perceived moments in order to live them in the
plenitude of their precariousness.

.

Maybe *The Book of Questions* is the question made
book.

No answer—no matter how persuasive—will ever
have enough strength to resist indefinitely the question that sooner or later will summon it.

An idea so sure of itself that it would no longer take
into account other ideas is dead before it is born.

Today, more so than in the past, to accept noth-

ing—even provisionally—that has not already some-
what resisted its systematic questioning should be a
basic principle.

The question has always been, is, and will remain
our best political weapon.

All acceptance is linked to the answer. May it never
for a moment become unconditional.

True solidarity has the question as guarantee.

I have interrogated you—he said. And for the duration
of my questioning, we were, both of us, o my brother,
only the vertigo of an infinite question put to ourselves.

Maybe the desert is the pulverized beyond of the
question: at the same time its disproportionate hu-
miliation and triumph.

There is no goal that, at the very moment it is reached,
is not already surpassed.

.

Identity is the name. Four letters were enough for
God—*Dieu*—to be God. Man—*l'homme*—needed five,
one of which is double.

What does that mean? Well, it means simply that
language deprives us of identity by offering us an identity that is but an assemblage of letters belonging only
to it and that we find again dispersed all over.

The letter is anonymous. It is a sound and a sign.
By participating in the formation of the name, it
creates, through it, our image. It then ceases to be
anonymous and becomes one with us. It espouses our
condition or our uncondition, lives and dies from our
life and from our death.

He who summons us, summons it first.

But is it a question of the letter or its reflection?

Its reflection, no doubt. In that case, our name would only be the reflection of an absence of the name that that absence itself would have composed. Thus our absence to the world our name answers for; thus our presence to the absent being whose name we have inherited.

The letter is to being what memory is to forgetting: at the same time the unscrolling of its history and the seal of its eternal sleep.

Translation by Pierre Joris

The Book of Questions
(1963)

AT THE THRESHOLD OF THE BOOK

Mark the first page of the book with a red marker. For, in the beginning, the wound is invisible.

—Reb Alcé

"What is going on behind this door?"

"A book is shedding its leaves."

"What is the story of the book?"

"Becoming aware of a scream."

"I saw rabbis go in."

"They are privileged readers. They come in small groups to give us their comments."

"Have they read the book?"

"They are reading it."

"Did they happen by for the fun of it?"

"They foresaw the book. They are prepared to encounter it."

"Do they know the characters?"

"They know our martyrs."

"Where is the book set?"

"In the book."

"Who are you?"

"I am the keeper of the house."

"Where do you come from?"

"I have wandered."

"Is Yukel your friend?"

"I am like Yukel."

"What is your lot?"

"To open the book."

"Are you in the book?"

"My place is at the threshold."

"What have you tried to learn?"

"I sometimes stop on the road to the sources and question the signs, the world of my ancestors."

"You examine recaptured words."

"The nights and mornings of the syllables which are mine, yes."

"Your mind is wandering."

"I have been wandering for two thousand years."

"I have trouble following you."

"I, too, have often tried to give up."

"Do we have a tale here?"

"My story has been told so many times."

"What is your story?"

"Ours, insofar as it is absent."

"I do not understand."

"Speaking tortures me."

"Where are you?"

"In what I say."

"What is your truth?"

"What lacerates me."

"And your salvation?"

"Forgetting what I said."

"May I come in? It is getting dark."

"In each word there burns a wick."

"May I come in? It is getting dark around my soul."

"It is dark around me, too."

"What can you do for me?"

"Your share of luck is in yourself."

"Writing for the sake of writing does nothing but show contempt."

"Man is a written bond and place."

"I hate what is said in places I have left behind."

"You trade in the future, which is immediately translated. What you have left is you without you."

"You oppose me to myself. How could I ever win this fight?"

"Defeat is the price agreed on."

"You are a Jew, and you talk like one."

"The four letters JUIF which designate my origin are your four fingers. You can use your thumb to crush me."

"You are a Jew, and you talk like one. But I am cold. It is dark. Let me come into the house."

"There is a lamp on my table. And the house is in the book."

"So I will live in the house after all."

"You will follow the book, whose every page is an abyss where the wing shines with the name."

AND YOU SHALL BE IN THE BOOK

When, as a child, I wrote my name for the first time, I knew I was beginning a book.

—Reb Stein

("*What is light?*" *one of his disciples asked Reb Abbani.*

"*In the book,*" *replied Reb Abbani, "there are unsuspected large blank spaces. Words go there in couples, with one single exception: the name of the Lord. Light is in these lovers' strength of desire.*

"*Consider the marvelous feat of the storyteller, to bring them from so far away to give our eyes a chance.*"

And Reb Hati: "The pages of the book are doors. Words go through them, driven by their impatience to regroup, to reach the end of the work, to be again transparent.

"*Ink fixes the memory of words to the paper.*

"*Light is in their absence, which you read.*")

Do I know, at this hour when men lift their eyes up to the sky, when knowledge claims a richer, more beautiful part of the imagination (all the secrets of the universe are buds of fire soon to open), do I know, in my exile, what has driven me back through tears and time, back to the wells of the desert where my ancestors had ventured? There is nothing at the threshold of the open page, it seems, but this wound of a race born of the book, whose order and disorder are roads of suffering. Nothing but this pain, whose past and whose permanence is also that of writing.

The word is bound to the word, never to man, and the Jew to his Jewish world. The word carries the weight of each of its letters, as the Israelite has, from the first dawn, carried that of his image.

Water marks the boundaries of oases. Between one tree and another, there is all the thirst of the earth.

"I am the word. And you claim to know me by my face," said Reb Josué, one day, to a rabbi come to meet him, indignant that the inspired man should be known by his features.

A town at night is a shopwindow emptied of things.

A few graffiti on a wall were enough for the dormant memories in my hand to take over my pen, for my fingers to determine what I see.

The story of Sarah and Yukel is the account, through various dialogues and meditations attributed to imaginary rabbis, of a love destroyed by men and by words. It has the dimensions of the book and the bitter stubbornness of a wandering question.

> *("The soul is a moment of light, which the first word can touch off. Then we are like the universe with thousands of heavenly bodies on our skin. You know them apart by the intensity of their radiance, as you tell a star by the clarity of its avowal."*
>
> —Reb Aber
>
> *"Distance is light, as long as you keep in mind that there are no limits.*
> *"We are distance."*
>
> —Reb Mirshak)

.

He writes.

He writes for the sake of his hand, his pen, to appease his eyes. For if he did not write, what would become of them? His pen would be unusable by now, choked with rust. His hand unreflected in any word, any letter. It would not have formed any image in ink. As for his eyes, they would have foundered on the page closed to them, uninvited at any moment of their passage. Only writing can keep the writer's eyes on the surface.

He follows the course of his eyes. He questions. He does not have the time to answer. So many questions turn away from his tongue, race along his arm towards his palm. So many desires push the pen, give his fingers the strength to push the pen.

Where is the path? It must each time be discovered anew. A blank sheet is full of paths. You know you must go from left to right. You know there will be much walking, much effort. And always from left to right. You know beforehand (at least sometimes) that once the page is black with signs you will tear it up. You will walk the same way ten times, a hundred times: the pathway of your nose, of your neck, of your mouth, the pathway of your forehead, and of your soul. All these ways have their own ways. Else they would not be ways.

Having our paths (or our possible paths) mapped out for us, why do we usually take the one which leads us away from our goal, leads us elsewhere, where we are not? But perhaps we are there also? Only when guided by inspiration do we choose right, when we are receptive, in a state of grace. But that is rare, even very rare. And those who are (in the state of grace) do not know it. I mean, at the time. The more so, since being in the state of grace often means losing your way, your usual way, in order to follow another: more secret, more mysterious.

We all have our routes mapped out. And, on the unfolded map of knowledge, the longest are the shortest. He had experienced this recently. One afternoon, he had ventured into the desert which spreads in the East, beyond the frontiers of the Middle Eastern country where his parents lived. He needed a landscape to fit his loneliness. He drove his car in various directions. He plunged in to the limits of safety. Around him, a warm night took off her bracelets and necklaces.—The most amazing one was pink.—He marveled that she seemed to appear and disappear, multiply and, suddenly, become so small he could hold her in his arms. He admired the night for being a woman and a whole female world, for being naked and dressed in stars.

Now and then, the wind softly brushed over the shadow and its bed, furtively, like a scout, and was gone again. Nothing indicated with what violence it would, by sunrise, attack that particle of the void where he had taken refuge. Nothing. For up to that very moment, the sand did not drop its indifference.

—But perhaps that is exactly why?

At noon, he found himself facing the infinite, the blank page. All tracks, footprints, paths were gone. Buried. He had pitched a tent on arriving: how come it had not blown off? From inside, he watched the complex improvisations of the wind. He heard how it suddenly laughed with the sand, danced with the sand, amused and irritated the sand, amused itself and got irritated with the number of grains. And finally, it became, in its desire, a mad sand god dragging monstrous winged creatures off to conquer the world.

He was probably only a few dozen miles from his point of departure. But he did not know. And how could one, here, speak of arrival or departure? Everywhere: oblivion, the unmade bed of absence, the wandering kingdom of dust.

Man's salvation is whatever has, as he has, a beginning and an end, whatever can start over. Salvation is the water that quenches our thirst only to be needed again. It is the bread which satisfies and maintains our hunger. It is what sprouts, develops, ripens for man and with him. Eternity, the infinite, are enemies of pulp and rind. When there is nothing left, there will still be sand. There will still be the desert to conjugate the nothing.

In the heart of what no longer is moved nor takes root, in the heart of the self-contained that defies reason and seasons (the keys of the desert surrender the five continents), in the heart of these arid stretches which repelled the sea as slowness overcame them (slowness is a formidable power: it has the passion of immobility with which it will, some day, fuse), in the heart of the irrevocable refusal to be (because living means acknowledging one's limits) man is like a prisoner in jail: he is finally conscious of his loss, the victory of his loss. What can you do against a wall? You tear it down. What can you do against bars? You file them. But a wall of sand? Bars which are shadows on sand? When the goal is always yet farther away, there is no advance.

The infinite has the transparency of evil. Whatever goes beyond us despises us. Whatever escapes us destroys us. Wherever the birds fly low in order to see their shape, the sky has pushed off the dunes, and death set up reign, welcomed by the meek landmarks of death.

For all that, he was not in danger. He simply had to get back to the sea on foot. His car was no help, with its motor clogged by the sandstorm and its wheels bogged down.

He made a plan. He would start out at sundown. But until then? The heat was scorching. He decided to lie down in his tent. His head hurt. He would rest every two hours. He would trust his instinct for the direction and shortcuts.

March winds act like falcons which, if there are enough of them, knock you down after pecking out your eyes. He imagined a blind world, completely at their mercy. Would he find the beach, his house?

His heart beat regularly, as if a source were hollowing out a path through his chest. He clung to his heart, as if to hold on to the source. He clung to any symbol, any naive image of life. Poor man, he had no idea he was turning away from himself.

To recover, after each blow, the original balance of life and death, to sacrifice to one as to the other, to one after the other, to be dead with death and living with life up to your last sigh (which is not death's triumph, but forsaking the body): this is health.

As an adolescent he had gone through the first, painful apprenticeship of death. He had seen it close by. He had stood at its bedside. Death speaks our language. In order to be understood it comes down to our level—or lifts us up to the level of catastrophe, and even lends us its own voice. Bending over his sister's bed, he had heard her going much beyond his juvenile revolt, revealing to him the far side of things, the territory of chance.

To answer the dying girl he had used, as she had, words prompted by death—the only ones which could unite them. When they fell silent, he understood that he had lost her.

Likewise with leaves and with sand. The dialogue cannot, must not be interrupted. Dialogue of the living with the leaves—dialogue of the dead with the sand.

He let go, by and by. Death had become his task. He entered into the system which is the condition of existence. He discovered its close and precise functioning. Like the body, the soul needs to be taken care of. And the soul is hungry for the bread of life and death.

He remembered the answer Reb Aaron gave to a strange rabbi come to question his teaching:

"He who lives within himself, beside his God, beside the life and death of God, lives in two adjoining rooms with a door between. He goes from one to the other in order to celebrate Him. He goes from presence in consciousness to presence in absence. He must fully be, before he can aspire to not being any more, that is to say: to being more, to being all. For absence is All."

He died for each second. He gathered a strength from beyond the grave. He was a fraction of the desert and an inflection of the wind. He stripped the untouched page of its leaves.

But the word is a triumphant sower. Dawn and dusk are written, as is race. When he got back to his neighborhood, to his house (a nomad had taken him on his camel to the nearest control post, where he caught a military truck to town), so many words urged him. He was, however, bent on avoiding them. They were still too much in love with space for him to think of fixing them.

God rests in man,
as man rests under a tree.
And the shadow, by grace of God, is man
in the tree, and tree in man.

I could have been this man. I have shared his shadow.
"Yukel, tell us of the shadow we have in common."

("A shadow is never more than a shadow," said Reb
Hazel. But Ioakim Elia, who knew the origin of shad-
ows, did not like this inference.
"A shadow is never more than appearance," he
said. "But we know that the world, each morning,
scuttles itself to make room for appearance."
"But this world," replied Reb Hazel, "how can you
grasp it, if it does not exist?"
"I can grasp what I see," said Ioakim Elia. "I only
have to open or close my eyes.")

"Have you thought," said Reb Sia to his New Year's guests, "of
the importance of the shadow? It is reflection and the sacrifice of
reflection. It is man's double and negation. It is also a cool oasis.
"But do not confuse shadow with gutted light. For shadow is at
the same time focus of light and dead language."
And the first guest answered:
"I have thought of it, thanks to you, master. I am now a shadow.
I have kept my body. I have my eyes, my mouth. I hear my heart
beat with my hand. And yet I hover, lighter than a feather. Is this
not wonderful?"

And the second guest answered:

"I have thought of it, thanks to you, master. I know now that death is not the loss of memory, but its apotheosis. An apotheosis of light. You no longer need to make an effort to remember. You see all the way back to childhood. You are reduced to eye and ear, as at the theater. This makes me wonder: does the audience at these secular stage amusements know that a play is an apprenticeship and that, in those amusing, moving, or disconcerting hours, they learn, passively, to die."

And the third guest answered:

"I have thought of it, thanks to you, master. When, as a child, I passed you and one of your disciples in the street, I said to myself: 'It must be like this when shadows talk.' Your pallor, your frozen smile, your lack of vitality were the origin of all my thinking."

"What you took for lack of vitality is, on the contrary, vitality at its apex," Reb Sia replied. And he added:

"The man crazy about writing dreams of being a shadow in order to marry the water. From this union, books are born.

"But the shadow is only a spot of memory, perceived by the eye.

"Our memory of God (which grows as we keep His law) transforms the believer into an abundant fig tree known by the rustling of its leaves and its peculiar scent.

"The shadow is place and becoming of God on the implacable path of the light."

I could have been this shadow. I have shared its daring.

"Yukel, tell us the exploits of your shadow."

"I will tell you the story of Nathan Seichell."

In the ghetto, his name is revered. He lives among his people like a fountain in a small square. He is quoted. He is treated with familiarity and yet with deference. He is also feared: people do not wish to displease him. The most beautiful room is for Nathan Seichell: an abandoned nook, furnished by the imagination, most comfortable (so people are persuaded). And on Passover? On Passover, he eats on silver plates with engraved borders, borrowed from the Cohn family, which is, rightly, proud of them.

For some, Nathan is the sage outside time, the seer to consult. Women discuss him among themselves:

"And you know what Nathan said to me?"

"You will have a son who will drink at the breast of night. He will grow like an olive tree watered by your tears."

"Will my son not be born from my womb? You worry me, Nathan. Why will I cry so much?"

"And you know what he said?"

"You will wallow in pain."

"But I will have had my joy."

"And you know what he said?"

"Joy, in the ghetto, is a candle. Hope, a conflagration."

Frightening, sometimes, as the Kabbalists were.—But he owes them nothing.

"At the origin, there is language. God is a circle of luminous letters. He is each of the letters of His Name. He is also the middle, the void of the circle where man and the woman about to be mother stand.

"Confronted with one of the divine letters—the circle broken— the creature recognized by its own sign will bear its mark."

"You believe in chance, Nathan?"

"Chance is the explanation people give to those unforeseen encounters which upset their lives. Chance is no business of God's. He does not try to explain. Adonai is. And everything is, in its hour, around Him, through Him.

"Thus, we know only a part of Adonai, the part which appeared to us in a steady flash of lightning.—In movement, His name, like Himself, is rebellious light.

"Thus, we know only a part of our Lord. It gives us access to the All beyond knowledge.

"Our life, in its good aspects, has the form of a revealed letter. The sounds which gave birth to it reverberate within us.

"Our life, in its evil aspects, has the form of an upside down letter, excluded from the Book of Books because it is illegible."

And Nathan added further:

"Aie . . . Aie . . . The groans of the Jewish people are in the body of the Eternal."

For others, Nathan is the disinterested companion who puts his experience at the disposal of the community.

"Who gave you this advice?"

"Nathan."

Nothing is begun without his approval. If he turns out to be wrong, he was misunderstood.

At any reunion, he is the guest of honor. And in the synagogue (the walls of the humblest synagogue are immense pieces of sky) his voice drowns out the voice of whole worlds.

"Mommy, tell me about Nathan Seichell."

Every child wants to drink his mother's words of truth. And the mother perpetuates the legends.

"Boys," she says, "always have a thousand tricks up their sleeves. But Nathan was different. Not that he was above games. He just never seemed altogether present."

"Nathan, you are so absent-minded it will ruin you."

"It saves me," he replied. "It will save us all."

"Look here," his uncle David countered. "Since when does one defend one's interests by turning one's back?"

One morning, a little before noon, his older sister had gone to meet him as she did every day, when she suddenly saw him appear in the light in front of her. (She was so startled she froze on the spot.) She saw him wave at her before disappearing: first one arm, then the other, the legs then, and finally the face, as if between two ocean waves. But he did not seem to struggle.—Was she in the street? Was she living a nightmare? She tried to cry for help, but her voice had no sound, it was stretched out under her. She waited, helpless, to get it back, waited for someone to help her voice pull itself together and give it back to her. In vain. Her heart carried her off toward the open sea. She knew she would never again reach port.

"Nathan, you are so absent-minded it will cost you your life."

Immediately after, a rumor spread through the ghetto that Nathan, son of Rachel, had drowned in his soul (his clothes bore witness on the spot where they had been left) and that his sister was rocked by the waves, just as the faithful in prayer seem to be standing, but are really on their backs.

(We think they are standing because we cannot imagine them otherwise. With their shawls around their shoulders they are, in fact, boats at the mercy of wind and sea. At the hours of service the waves come,

sometimes so big they shake the synagogue. Leaving
the synagogue is a real landing. You return to your
street, your family, as after a rewarding absence.)

"I knew it would happen," screamed his uncle David. "Now Nathan is walking around naked."

But all the others around uncle David begged:

"Nathan, Nathan, show yourself."

"Are you here, there?"

"Are you before, behind us?"

"Are you up there?"

"Are you down beneath?"

"We all have been lost in ourselves, but the others could see and touch us."

"Nathan, let us see you, and we will lead you back to the earth."

At that point, a voice was heard. Indistinct at first (miracles are not reassuring the moment they happen), then clearer and clearer as they got used to it (to get used to a miracle means forgetting it—hence, everything is a miracle). A voice of flesh and sparkling scales. A voice was seen exhibiting its words:

"I am luminous like the dialogue on the seven-armed candelabra in the synagogue, on both sides of the chest with the parchments of the Law about which a poet said that, unrolled, they are the shores of the kingdom of God. But I am shadow, crest and abyss of shadow."

The crowd was getting larger and more excited. They begged:

"Let us see you, Nathan."

"Let us see you."

The voice went on:

"I am what solicits and separates, limits and unfolds. I am the second presence."

People were so worked up that it worried the outsiders. Alerted soldiers entered the ghetto, weapon in hand, to reestablish order. The agitators would be judged and punished. Seichell's older sister would be the first to be dragged by her hair before the tribunal.— But who could catch her in the middle of the ocean?

As the soldiers attacked the protesting crowd with increasing violence, the following happened: pushed back without knowing how or by whom, kept apart from their victims just when they thought of striking, they hit the empty air with their sabres. And the emptiness spread and settled among them. The soldiers were blinded with flowing blood, but not a single ghetto dweller was hurt. The empty air bled. Also the soldiers: they could not avoid their own swords.

The ghetto was like an island, its outline defined, through the arm of Nathan Seichell, by the inhabitants' anger, stubbornness, faith, and love.

"This is the story," concluded the mother.

Men of my race develop in a cocoon. They are locked inside their fears and convictions. They belong to the family of silkworms (night silkworms) and of fish, whose cocoon is the ocean.

Every Jew drags behind himself a scrap of the ghetto, a scrap of rescued land where he takes refuge when alarmed. His chains isolate him from the world. But the chains fall when Jews are among themselves.

Cursed land, received like the promised land. Solitary land— semblance of a land—with the color of hope.

Lavish absence.

("*Events half open for us the door of a gallery of mirrors where we see ourselves at all ages. They show within us long halls of idealized and occasional portraits.*

"*We draw courage from their example,*" *said Reb Silon.*

"*Look at these people,*" *said Reb Mathias.* "*They are wells chased away from their water. When their step gets heavier, they have recaptured their land.*")

The Jew answers every question with another question.

—Reb Léma

My name is a question. It is also my freedom within my tendency to question.

—Reb Eglal

"Our hope is for knowledge," said Reb Mendel. But not all his disciples were of this opinion.

"We first have to agree on the sense you give to the word 'knowledge,'" said the oldest of them.

"Knowledge means questioning," answered Reb Mendel.

"What will we get out of these questions? What will we get out of all the answers which only lead to more questions, since questions are born of unsatisfactory answers?" asked the second disciple.

"The promise of a new question," replied Reb Mendel.

"There will be a moment," the oldest disciple continued, "when we have to stop interrogating. Either because there will be no answer possible, or because we will not be able to formulate any further questions. So why should we begin?"

"You see," said Reb Mendel: "at the end of an argument, there is always a decisive question unsettled."

"Questioning means taking the road to despair," continued the second disciple. "We will never know what we are trying to learn."

"True knowledge is daily awareness that, in the end, one learns nothing. The Nothing is also knowledge, being the reverse of the All, as the air is the reverse of the wing."

"Our hope is the wings of despair. For how would we progress otherwise?" replied Reb Mendel.

"Intelligence," said the third disciple, "is more dangerous than the heart, which relies only on its own beat. Who among us can assert that he is right?"

"Only the hope to be right is real. Truth is the void," replied Reb Mendel.

"If the truth which is in man is void," continued the oldest disciple, "we are nothing in a body of flesh and skin. Therefore God, who is our truth, is also nothing?"

"God is a question," replied Reb Mendel. "A question which leads us to Him who is Light through and for us, who are nothing."

Our meeting, this evening, is about to end. The story I promised you is in your memory. Our passage across pact and imposture, across soul and hands without echo, has led us, via telling detours, to our eyes. They will understand and judge what they see in terms of what they have seen. Both truth and justice are incorruptible eyes: the innocent eyes of the child.

They see freedom in the distance.

THE TIME OF THE LOVERS

Yukel: A blank page swarms with steps on the point of finding their own tracks. An existence is a scrutiny of signs.

Sarah: Is the dream not already death, Yukel? You bet on the margins, the clouds. Man carries time. We play against. Time is becoming, a second's blaze rekindled.

Yukel: Man is a merchant of ashes. Out of the world, I save the moment, my portion of eternity.
Sarah, my moment, my eternity.

Sarah: The word cancels out distance, drives space to despair. Is it really we who formulate it, or does it, rather, mold us?

Yukel: The hours tell man that he advances, whether lying down or standing, that he turns in circles like the hands of the clock—unaware that they are turning.
Daughters of the moon in their worry to light up a few inches of the universe, a fraction of the infinite, however minute, they have the coquetry of their sex and the jealousy of a jailer.
This morning, the hour was sublime light. The sun had mastered the dark. I had gotten up before dawn to witness a victory no doubt counted on, but unpredictable in its details. I watched the dismantling of the night, the capture of every single trench of shadow. What unsuspected cunning. What snares prepared in secret.
Words are windows, doors half open onto space. I divine their presence by their pressure against our palms, by the imprint they leave there.

Sarah: The sun conjugates life, in its visible diversion, through all the moods. Lovers prefer the night. They recognize each other by the shadow they bathe in like swimmers whose every muscle is caressed into hymns. At the bottom of the water, the heart is heard more clearly.

Yukel: Where are you, Sarah? My lady without manor, my river without banks. Your body does not hold you any more.

Sarah: I wrote you. I write you. I wrote you. I write you. I take refuge in my words, the words my pen weeps. As long as I am speaking, as long as I am writing, my pain is less keen. I join with each syllable to the point of being but a body of consonants, a soul of vowels. Is it magic? I write his name, and it becomes the man I love. All it takes to pass from night to day, and from day to night, is that a pen dipped in ink obey the movement of my hand, that the voice yield for a second to the whim of the lips, to the orders of thought. I hollow out a dwelling in desire. I write: "I am going to join you, my love . . ." And, instantly, I am wings which give me back my beloved. I say: "Be patient, my love . . ." and let the walls of my prison take me in again.

Yukel: I wrote you. I write you. I wrote you. I write you. I give you pet names, my little bird. I see you again in my hotel room, so upset by my departure. "Why? Why?" you pleaded. I see you again that last evening, some indifferent square between us. I see you running across the street between my hotel and your place. It is so dark.

Sarah: I wrote you. I write you. I wrote you. I write you. Write me, my love. I have lain in wait for the mailman all day long, as usual. Put my face on your avowals, chisel my shape in words. I am beautiful because I am the words which enhance me through your mouth. I am pale because your sadness lies on my cheeks. You write: "Your fingers are the paintbrush of my hope." And my fingers grow, in their delight. You compare my arms to young waterfalls, my neck to a nest of timid birds, and I am water coming down the mountain, I am the cooing of the air imprisoned in its heart. My eyes open when you look at them. My breasts harden at your touch. Come, my beloved. Walk at my speed. We are our road.

Yukel: We move in ourselves, as the moon in the gold of its fine skin, as the current in the laugh of the river. Entangled, we are our universe. I had not thought our bodies were so vast, so deep. On the surface, they are two lovers: you and me. One can see them, talk to them. They do not take up much room. They cast a shadow in the morning. But enter into them, and they are giants the gods quarrel over. Beside itself, a being dwindles, draws in.

We are immense, Sarah. I am walking by your side.

Sarah: I write: "We are the signs gathered by our hands, the sounds uttered by our lips," and all of a sudden, a comma seems the image of a sigh, a full stop a border. We go from one sentence to the next, from one paragraph to the next, without realizing the number of miles covered.

Yukel: You are by my side, Sarah. I am swaying in the hammock woven by your perfume, slung from the dry branches of oblivion.

Sarah: I am the spring of oblivion. Lakes take our measure, like mirrors.

Where are you, Yukel? Words stick to my flesh as to blotting paper.

The world is illegible on the skin.

·

(The sleeping quarters of screams stretch beyond echo's reach. Formerly, one only heard screams when they awoke. And it happened that they slept a long time. Nowadays, they no longer sleep at all.

One day, before he died, the shaved rabbi who, in his deportation clothes, no longer looked like a rabbi, said to me:
"What is the water in a lake? A blank page. The ripples are its wrinkles. And every one is a wound.
"A lake without ripples is a mirror. A wrinkled lake is a face."
"In their markings, our faces reflect God's."

I turned to the rabbi and answered:
"You lie. What about the face of the innocent?"

The rabbi turned to me and explained:
"The wrinkles of the innocent are ripples a breeze sketches and undoes as it subsides.
"Wonder is a twinkle of the skin.
"God is in the slightest shiver."

I turned to the rabbi and said:
"God is in the wind, Rabbi, in the wind which wreaks havoc."

And the rabbi interrupted me:
"Do not blaspheme, Yukel. If the tree is a tree, it is because it has never blasphemed. Each of its knots is a bond.")

So we are brothers in our faces.

Here, elsewhere; elsewhere, here: a glass block, a ball.

The globe is pulverized by its reflections. In the sun, you can admire their variety. All the fond shades of men—and of the things enumerated in their eyes. There are blue and red reflections. There is the yellow reflection, the green. The yellow will never turn blue, nor the green red.

"Our breast is a jail," wrote Reb Veda. "Our ribs are the bars which keep us from suffocating.

"You will live in your jail, brother, for your salvation. The elect is a prisoner of the transmitted word of God. For its survival, he makes his body into a cell fitting the word.

"You will know the happiness of being inhabited by your God."

To which Reb Sia replied:

"The happiness to be oneself is what the horse feels when it has thrown off its rider.

"But the earth I tread is infested with snakes. Accept me, Lord, as your mount. And let us together run across the starry infinite which unfolds through you."

THE BOOK OF THE LIVING

The light of Israel is a scream to the infinite.

The fence can be seen from afar. The house, with its roof (which the clouds fear because it looks deceptively like a cloud), with its closed doors and windows, looks out over the madwoman's path, which no one else walks.

"That madwoman," asked Sarah, "is she really dead?"

"The scream you heard was an owl. Let's go back in. It's late."

The women in the village made the sign of the cross. The men fell silent long enough to identify the scream and shrug.

"There she goes again."

"There she goes again."

The fence can be seen from afar. It is in flower. The seasons are born and die in the ground.

"There she goes again," said Léonie Lull, turning her head towards the hill. "There she goes again.

"Even in my sleep I hear her."

"Even when she does not scream, I hear her," said Mathilde Meyvis.

The madwoman's house sleeps in its cradle rocked by the nurse's hands. The madwoman's house rocks amid trees hidden by their leaves.

We have to cut off the hands,
    have to fell the trees
to destroy the madwoman's house in its cradle.
    We must wake her.

The water you float on, the water you give in to, is the water of sleep.

The water you wash in, the water you fight against, is the water
of awakening.

Madness keeps awake
the madwoman's sleep,
but never wakes her.

The madwoman sleeps and moves, makes gestures and sleeps
(makes her sleep make gestures), speaks and sleeps (makes her sleep
speak).

"There she goes again."
"There she goes again."

"That madwoman," asked Sarah, "is she really dead?"

"As the dark is pierced by the light, the soul is pierced by the
scream," wrote Reb Seriel.
And Reb Louel: "The Jewish soul is the fragile casket of a scream."

Madness keeps awake
the madwoman's sleep,
but never wakes her.

"That owl," asked Sarah, "is it really me?"
"The scream you heard was an owl. Let's go back in. It's late."

"I do not hear the scream," said Sarah. "I am the scream."

> *(The lives of one or two generations of men may fill
> one sentence or two pages. The gross outline of four
> particular or ordinary lives: "He was born in . . . He
> died in . . ." Yes, but between the scream of life and
> the scream of death? "He was born in . . . He was in-
> sulted for no good reason . . . He was misunderstood
> . . . He died in . . ." Yes, but there must be more? "He
> was born in . . . He tried to find himself in books . . .
> He married . . . He had a son . . . He died in . . ."*

Yes, yes, but there must be more? "He was born on
. . . He gave up books . . . He thought he would live
on in his son . . . He died on . . ." *Yes, but there must
be more?* "He was short and heavy-set . . . He had a
childhood and an old age . . . His name was Salomon
Schwall . . ." *Yes, yes, but there must be more?* "His
name was Salomon Schwall . . . He does not remember his youth . . . He left his island . . . He went to
Portugal . . . His wife was called Léonie . . ." *Yes,
yes, but there must be more?* "He settled in the South
of France with his wife . . . He was an antique dealer
. . . He was called 'the Jew' . . . His wife and son were
called 'the wife and the son of the Jew.'" *Yes, but there
must be more?* "He died, and his wife died . . . They
were buried in ground which did not know their
names, near some crosses . . ." *Yes, but there must be
more?* "His son was French . . . He fought in the war
for France . . . He was decorated . . ." *Yes, yes, but
there must be more?* "He fought in the infantry . . .
was wounded . . . decorated . . ." *Yes, yes, but there
must be more?* "He was still called 'the Jew' . . . He
married Rebecca Sion, whom he met in Cairo . . . He
went back to France with her . . ." *Yes, but there
must be more?* "He became a merchant in memory of
his father . . . He had brought back all sorts of objects
from his travels . . . Oceanic and African masks . . .
pottery and gemstones from China, carved ivory from
Japan . . ." *Yes, but there must be more?* "He had a
daughter, Sarah . . ." *Yes, but there must be more?*
"He was still called 'the Jew,' and his wife and daughter, 'the wife and the daughter of the Jew.'" *Yes, yes,
but there must be more?* "He had lost his faith . . . He
no longer knew who he was . . . He was French . . .
decorated . . . His wife and daughter were French
. . ." *Yes, but there must be more?* "Sometimes, he
spoke in public to brand racism, to affirm the rights
of man . . ." *Yes, yes, but there must be more?* "He
died in a gas chamber outside France . . . and his wife

died in a gas chamber outside France . . . and his
daughter came back to France, out of her mind . . .")

The madwoman's house sleeps in its cradle, rocked by the nurse's hands. The madwoman's house rocks amid trees hidden by their leaves.
 We have to cut off the hands,
 have to fell the trees
to destroy the madwoman's house in its cradle.
 We must wake her.

"One is the only one to know one's life," said Moses Schwall. "And one's life is a breath."

"The owl howling against the wind," asks Sarah, "is it me, Yukel, is it me? The owl against the wind, the owl for the wind? Is it me, Yukel, is it me? The wind sweeping off my screams, my screams exasperating the wind?"

·

Have you seen how a word is born and dies?
Have you seen how two names are born and die?
From now on, I am alone.
The word is a kingdom.
Every letter has its quality, its grounds, and its rank. The first holds the greatest power, power of fascination and obsession. Omnipotence is its lot.
Sarah.
Yukel.
United kingdoms, innocent worlds, which the alphabet conquered and then destroyed through the hands of men.
You have lost your kingdom.
I have lost my kingdom, as my brothers have, scattered everywhere in a world which has feasted on their dispersion.
Have you seen how a kingdom is made and unmade?
Have you seen how a book is made and unmade?

The Book of Yukel
(1964)

WHITE SPACE

"I would, at the end of my life, like to keep one part of my childish habit of stubbornly hitting stone with my naked fist: the vision of the infinite white of the wall."

—Reb Ara

1

And Yukel said:

"Is this not the day when suffering took the shape of a fist?

"This fist is no menace. It is worn down by the wall. In vain it hit the unfeeling thickness of walls.

"It is clear that fist and groan are related.

"They have the same origin.

"Reb Sideva reminded us we have wept so much over the centuries that to each of our tears there corresponds the brief twinkling of a star.

"A drop of water sometimes contains more light than an egg of fire. We have molded our sun in pain, with our own fingers. We have hard skin, but burned blood.

"'Fierce flames of my heart,' wrote Reb Seba, 'almost a fireplace by which I dream an animal dream.' And Reb Abber: 'Our sun is black. Do not wonder. We put it out for a moment which has lasted millennia. Tomorrow, we will be warm.'

"Our bread will be white."

2

"Reb Akri's thinking," said Reb Jaffa, "irritates me on more than one count. I must admit, however, that his study of the natural, our first level, intrigues me.

"I have spent my life looking for the base and have not succeeded in placing it in relation to the top. Is it straw of the deep or mesh, the chosen exile of the peak?"

"I was caught in the net of pinnacles as the sun is in the net of morning. God is the Fisher."

—Reb Mazaltov

3

"Time was heavy.
We weighed the same,
wished for the same heights."

—Reb Nadir

"I rise, but way up there is my soul trying to rise still higher."
—Reb Nefla

"Behind the sun, a yet lonelier sky."

—Reb Bar

4

"Silence is the kernel of noise. Therefore, God, who is hard silence, cannot be heard, only accepted as the fruit colors are accepted by the hours of the tree."

—Reb Guesin

"The soul's vocabulary is that of wing and dewdrop. It is flight and heavenly brew."

—Reb Naam

"My soul, you move in words as day moves in gestures of gold. I speak. Is this not proof that you exist?"

—Reb Sayod

"God is after life, where life changes its name."

—Reb Feder

"God is the incandescent point facing the dark point of the written page. For to man's book of nights corresponds God's blinding book of light."

—Reb Sari

5

"The future is the past coming."

—Reb Evné

"You came and saw. Now, the world is in your eyes."

—Reb Ibil

"Lie down for an instant. How else would you know you are walking?"

—Reb Eken

"Yesterday is not the problem. I was born the day before."

—Reb Nalag

"Always is in all, in all ways."

—Reb Kaloun

"I heard with Your ears and since have not stopped hearing You.
"I saw with Your eyes and since have not stopped seeing You.
"I spoke with Your mouth and since have not stopped naming You.
"O Lord, for every minute
"You are the minute doubled."

—Reb Garam

MIRROR AND SCARF

*"We will gather images and images of images up till the
last, which is blank. This one we will agree on."*
—Reb Carasso

Mardohai Simhon claimed the silk scarf he wore around his neck
was a mirror.

"Look," he said, "my head is separated from my body by a scarf.
Who dares give me the lie if I say I walk with a knotted mirror under
my chin?

"The scarf reflects a face, and you think it is of flesh.

"Night is the mirror. Day the scarf. Moon and sun reflected features. But my true face, brothers, where did I lose it?"

At his death, a large scar was discovered on his neck.

The meaning of this anecdote was discussed by the rabbis.

Reb Alphandery, in his authority as the oldest, spoke first.

"A double mirror," he said, "separates us from the Lord so that
God sees Himself when trying to see us, and we, when trying to see
Him, see only our own face."

"Is appearance no more than the reflections thrown back and forth
by a set of mirrors?" asked Reb Ephraim. "You are no doubt alluding
to the soul, Reb Alphandery, in which we see ourselves mirrored.
But the body is the place of the soul, just as the mountain is the bed
of the brook. The body has broken the mirror."

"The brook," continued Reb Alphandery, "sleeps on the summit.
The brook's dream is of water, as is the brook. It flows for us. Our
dreams extend us.

"Do you not remember this phrase of Reb Alsem's: 'We live out
the dream of creation, which is God's dream. In the evening our own
dreams snuggle down into it like sparrows in their nests.'

"And did not Reb Hames write: 'Birds of night, my dreams explore the immense dream of the sleeping universe.'"

"Are dreams the limpid discourse between the facets of a crystal block?" continued Reb Ephraim. "The world is of glass. You know it by its brilliance, night or day."

"The earth turns in a mirror. The earth turns in a scarf," replied Reb Alphandery.

"The scarf of a dandy with a nasty scar," said Reb Ephraim.

> ("*Words are inside breath, as the earth is inside time.*"
>
> —Reb Mares)

And Yukel said:

"The bundle of the Wandering Jew contains the earth and more than one star."

"Whatever contains is itself contained," said Reb Mawas.

The story I told you, as well as the commentaries it inspired, will be recorded in the book of the eye. The ladder urges us beyond ourselves. Hence its importance. But in a void, where do we place it?

> ("*God is sculpted.*"
> —Reb Moyal)

THE VOICE OF CLOSED EYES

The voice of closed eyes is slow, heavy, like the voice of
a woman awaking from a night of love. A voice like the slow
rising, the slow opening of the dark.

1

"One morning," recounted Reb Shem, "Reb Yahé, then still an adolescent, came to see me at home. His overexcitement and incoherence made a most painful impression on me. I tried, by speaking very slowly, by appealing indirectly to his memory, to make him express himself clearly. No use. I had the feeling he was reading a book from the wrong side, as the dead do, and only a mirror in his mouth could get his sentences back in order.

"So I handed him a rose from my garden and added: 'Son, there is an order and harmony in beings and things which we cannot break without risk of jeopardizing even their names. Can anything compare with this rose?'

"A few days later, Reb Yahé came again. In his hand, he held a flower like the one I had plucked for him. He gave it to me with the words: 'Master, my reason has come back. My soul has found again the proper order of its petals and perfume.'"

> (*"You dream of writing a book. The book is already*
> *written."*
>
> —Reb Zaidan)

2

"A city," said Reb Ammar one day to his younger son, "is a heart whose beat you can no longer hear.

"Get out of the city, and you will discover its secret hidden in the sand."

"How could I tear from the desert a confession the city has hidden from me?" the younger son asked back.

"No confession," continued Reb Ammar, "but the distressing cry of the sea which is in the stones, gagged with cement."

And Reb Telha: "You will cross the land of the fish with its pulverized salt islands and beaches in love with their wounds.

"You will cross the ocean which keeps gulls' wings on the surface for a mysterious dialogue of wild feathers and scales.

"Tomorrow is a day to be lived in hothouse silence, on this side of the anguished murmur of waves, from one end of exile to the other.

"Lightly, the crown floats down the stream, but this reign has neither end nor voice to stifle it."

And Reb Ava: "We live in the sea. Its bottom links us to the land.

"We are children of the sea who do not remember the water."

DIALOGUE OF STONE AND SAND

1

The world of stones is a world of disciplined roads. A black world with bold forays into the light.

World of tunnels with rails for wrinkles.

And we ride on our double doldrums, on plain pain.

> *("We ride," said Reb Zolé. "We have wheels. But who would suspect it from the way we walk?*
>
> *"When the Jew in prayer stands on tiptoe and comes down again, it is because he has taken a rough road, and the wheels of his faith respond.")*

The day of stones will break tomorrow.

I teach the way.

2

"Witness of my time. Time has whitened my temples."

"I am the white of gold. Gold turns blue when hidden. Wind is my youth."

"My youth blows inside me, but I resist. Old from my earliest days. And hard."

"Witness of my action. You are stone for citadels and careful sculptors. You are stone for bridges and dams."

"I am nameless stone. My name is in the living light inside me."

"I am sun grains sown by the sky."

"I am glum far from my lips, my hands. My words are in the ground. But rub my body, in love or in battle, and it sparks fire."

"I speak to absence, to the springs of rain. My speech reigns absolute."

"I am the immobile bond, the distance withheld."

"I am the forgotten bottom of the sea. I am the impossible dream of tired water. The sky has sand in its hair."

"I am the eye of the sea without sky or bottom, reduced to its name."

"I am the sea beyond the sea, wave broken by wave."

"I am a skyscraper."

"Where stone gives way to stone,
and sand to sand,
I am the offering of firstfruits."

"I am stone when faced with snow, with grass, but I am close to the grain of sand through sun and salt and the wind."

"You are stone, our evidence shows, and the evidence divides us as far back as our remotest origins."

THE LAMP GROWN COLD

*"The laws of dawn are not those of the lamp. The sun
speaks to the universe, the lamp to solitary man."*
—Reb Acrida

*"The law is the egg.
The law is wings."*

—Reb Nessim

"We are ruled by laws," said Reb Mazol. "The laws of freedom
are the strictest, along with the law of fasting."

And he added: "The laws of light are inspired by the laws of the
dark. What is good for one is also good for the other. We have studied
the dark and the day through their common voice and conclude that
opposites are one."

He also said: "I shall write the book of laws."

*("God of Laws, You are the God of air and water.
The law of the air is to soar, the law of water to soak."*
—Reb Akaf)

"Freedom is like the stem of a rose. Thorns announce the petals."
—Reb Galim

"To obey the laws of the universe—
to make green both back and front."

—Reb Taor

"Between dusk and dark—
between star and caste."

—Reb Timbah

And Yukel said:

> "The law is in the word.
> I write: I apply the law."

DIALOGUE OF THE FERRYMAN
AND THE RIVER-DWELLER

River-dweller: I cannot get to the other bank without your help. Ferryman, tell me of the other bank.

Ferryman: For me, it is the bank to get to, just like this one is when I am over there.

River-dweller: Is it like the banks of my childhood? It is so far I cannot tell from here.

Ferryman: What matter what the country is like if it excites your imagination. What matter what its banks are like. It is your country as long as you think of it, your banks.

River-dweller: I would like to know where this country begins and ends, if its vegetation is related to ours. The shape of its trees and rocks. I would like to know what happens there.

Ferryman: There is life, like here, and life in death. Like here, there is darkness in the light of the Name.

Return to the Book
(1965)

DEDICATION

In the cemetery of Bagneux, *département de la Seine*, rests my mother. In old Cairo, in the cemetery of sand, my father. In Milano, in the dead marble city, my sister is buried. In Rome where the dark dug out the ground to receive him, my brother lies. Four graves. Three countries. Does death know borders? One family. Two continents. Four cities. Three flags. One language: of nothingness. One pain. Four glances in one. Four lives. One scream.

Four times, a hundred times, a thousand times one scream.

"And those who were not buried?" asked Reb Azel.

"All the shadows in the world are screams," replied Yukel.

(Mother, I answer to life's first call, to the
first word of love, and the world has your voice.)

FORESPEECH

"God died with my childhood," wrote Reb Guebra. "He died with my youth. Now he is dying with me. In the eternal void, three fiery arrows thus recall a man's passing, perhaps his last questions?"

And Yukel said:

"Was Reb Guebra a good or bad rabbi? I could not judge. Did he, the student of Reb Asrot, betray his teacher? And did he, like those inspired men who were condemned for their bold ideas, commit the sacrilege of challenging the Law of God? If so, he no doubt deserved that people turn from him. And from me too, for of all the rabbis who have their place in the book Reb Guebra is most like me."

> *(And Reb Fehad told this story:*
> *"I mingled with a crowd of people and asked: Where is the Book?*
> *"A man in the crowd replied: I had it in my hands.*
> *"I went up to him and asked: Show me the Book.*
> *"The man laughed and said: I threw it into the river so the water could read it.*
> *"Then I said: Earth furnished the pages. Water and fire the writing.*
> *"Alas, the man was gone."*
> *And Reb Askol explained: "Both of you were words in the Book.")*

LIGHTNING AND LIGHT

*"God in man: but this means the impossibility of God
made possible every time the heart debates an overwhelming
delight."*
—Reb Elfié

"You are the space of poetry, I am its dead end."
—Reb Rimah

1

"Which people is more naked than the people of Israel? Purity
its only ornament."

—Reb Guetta

"If I told you that a rabbi's chant during the service gives us back
our land, would you believe me? Our world is a voice, a sob, a few
holy words."

—Reb Aleh

"I am, the tree calls to the tree, and the pebble to the simple
pebble."

—Reb Sahed

"You find it hard to speak of the book, and I, to speak of it to you.
The trouble is in the book."

—Reb Dérim

"You are my son. Your book will be the child of my book."
—Reb Acrim

2

"God owes to man His infinite chance to be Place."

—Reb Assar

"Revelation of God means revelation of man to the creature strain-
ing toward God; therefore we cannot recognize man without rec-
ognizing God.

"'*God is in prison*,' howled Reb Saharim in his death cell. However, the divine spirit survives man because death is the freedom of
God just as life, modeled on death, is the test of the freedom of man."

—Reb Sédad

"Death is the leveling absence of God."

—Reb Sabra

"We have little to say about many things. God had so much to say
about so little. God fell silent in the Void. Man chatters on in the
Fullness. But how will he make himself heard?"

—Reb Raccah

3

"The detours of thought cannot scare you. They borrow the ways
of our flesh."

—Reb Askri

"You comment on your commentary and so on and on until you
are the great-grandson of your own son."

—Reb Saber

"Sand attacking sand, leaf attacking leaf: is this not the order of
the seven seeds, the awakening at the approach of shores?

—Reb Elef

TEST AND BOOK

"I am a word-grain in the hidden field of Adonai."
—Reb Attal

"The soul has the resistance of the calf of a leg. I am down on the ground. You stomp on me. You stomp on my eternity."
—Reb Lehar

I have followed a book in its persistence, a book which is the story of a thousand stories as night and day are the prow of a thousand poems. I have followed it where day succeeds the night and night the day, where the seasons are four times two hundred and fifty seasons.

The world is exiled in the name. Within it there is the book of the world.

Writing means having a passion for origins. It means trying to go down to the roots. The roots are always the beginning. Even in death, no doubt, a host of roots form the deepest root bottom. So writing does not mean stopping at the goal, but always going beyond.

For five summers I have followed a book which advances quietly in the void where the work builds up. Daily enterprise of joining through the feverish page the ascus of the sign.

A book which is the lacing of risk.

I must tell a strange story which obsesses me of a woman in her eighties who, on her deathbed, spoke just before dying in the language of her childhood (which she had long forgotten). This act in the fog of the unconscious struck me—and still strikes me—as an example of the behavior of poets who speak in their works as they never do otherwise.

Every work cancels the dark. Every work is a hymn from the other side of memory to a memory that is spellbound. Beauty is death's gift to vulgar life so that it can live in beauty.

Abandoning one book means waiting impatiently for the next book's wish to come. The least weakness nails us to the spot.

Birds take wing from nests all around the blue sky. Their flight amazes me. The hour stays in our eyes. I wonder what wounds me without thinking of the wound. Seeing my blood I note that I have been bleeding.

I remember one late afternoon alone in the desert when I watched how the dark studded space with stars—with so fine a needle that I naively thought the sky must be full of wailing-women who at each stitch gave out a fiery scream. You could not say for sure if it was the scream of a woman in trance or of the pierced universe. I also re-member well how I first became aware of the gravity of silence: watching the Nile flow with its cargoes reminded me of an unbroken line of red ants, carrying their food. Hope made breath bolder. The world, all brightness, was dead to itself, was revealed to death in the most surprising lesson of life it had ever had. And I thought that a book ought to oscillate between these two silences, just as the tip of the pen should temper and bend it toward the words which people would read after God.

Any expression of knowledge is questioned by unfathomable oc-cult Powers, which even a mechanical movement, even the slightest murmur of thoughts or lips calls forth.

In the quest for the absolute which we pursue with our lesser means, questions periodically sacrifice us to their perennial life. We bear witness to their daring as washed-up pebbles to the adventure of the lake.

In this order, little by little, the book of days has opened into the book of infinite years; and I have participated in its slow but sure blossoming. I cannot imagine now that it could be taken from me. My life accompanies my death in the book; and the beings and things I am given to approach and appreciate are chosen, then lost and found again in other beings and new objects.

Proof is a prelude. The impetus toward God is a jump backward.

It is at any rate clear that we can justify a return to the past only in terms of the inescapable future which answers for it. The call of the roots does not reach the thorns or buds, but the rose in full bloom.

Thus every expected day is a day to live against the grain, a day to die. This double thrust of the centuries fulfills itself in the mental and cultural products of the ages for which we are seed and field.

Life and death have the same desire to last. Eternity knots them together.

In the book, the colors of the sea range from the ivory of absence to ink black. The sea bathes the shores I walk. In its shells I have heard the echo of my name moaning.

The Mediterranean has revived eyes before mine. This is why I want the sea to be the moving, millenary bond in the book. It is also why my dreams have the sense of a lifeline in a world torn with departures. Gangway! Down under there is perhaps a life for us.

Salt beds which the waves cannot lick, the Dead Sea is the very type of a ruined sea.

Not the slightest relation to the Mediterranean: morning sea, impulsive, but distracted, imaginative; amorous sea, soft; sea of swims and speed.

A handful of wheat in hunger betokens the union of men. A threatening fist clinches their drawing together. Love is in the gold of our fingers. The earth is the gold of love.

My trees are the flamboyant and the date tree. My flower is jasmine; my river the Blue Nile. My deserts, the sand and flint of Africa.

Do I have the right to consider them mine because they entered my pupils and my heart, and because my mouth trumpets them forth?

I am a man's wanderings, path and road. Had I so totally forgotten it? Calmly, resigned, and with manly consciousness I accepted the condition laid down: to wander through reality and the dream of reality for which every syllable of the book is a reason.

The word of God is not commandment but correspondence.

"What is the relation between reptile and rainbow?" asked Reb Behar one day of his teacher Reb Ephraim Sholem.

"A most subtle one," he answered: "the adumbration of a circle."

Sight often hides from us the deepest yearnings of free movement and innate gesture. For life is beyond, in the life which wakes.

So ever since the book my life has been a wake of writing in the space between limits, under the resplendent sign of the unpronounceable Name. A wake of besieged days and evenings. The world changes without knowing it. This long crossing merges with sleep.

Repetition is man's power to perpetuate himself in God's supreme speculations. To repeat the divine act in its First Cause. Thus man is God's equal in his power to choose an unpredictable Word which he alone can launch. I obey slavishly. I am master of the metamorphoses. Adventure is a property of words.

("God follows God, and Book follows Book."
—Reb Jorna)

HAND AND DIAL

"You will have truth as long as you tack within its
bounds."
——Reb Natié

"Whatever cannot be grasped is eternal."
——Reb Arifa

1

Associating with truth I appropriate its grounds and burn them. But where my property runs out, there stretches that of another truth, as exclusive, of which I could take possession if I wanted.

Thus I would circle the earth in order to die of my images. There are truths which rule over vast sunny estates. I would meet them all. For the time it takes to formulate a question I would take advantage of their sound company. I would adopt their reason and their perspective.

Back at my work table I would write up my travels. I would exploit the instruction I received; and my books would sound sincere. No one who read me would doubt my good faith—except myself: for back in my four walls, have I not been the host of a truth hostile to the others, a truth I cannot get rid of except by sacrificing it in the fire set by my discontent?

> *("He is a man of truth," said Reb Eloun about Reb*
> *Massé. "He walks on rugs of ashes."*
>
> *"God is the Truth of truths, the flowering flame*
> *within the flame.*
> ——Reb Férim)*

2

I am the breath of my books like wind engulfed by the sea. Every wave a suspension of foam and water; any color, the one the sky takes. But raising the waves, inventing their forms and fringes, the wind too is reborn and runs with them through the ocean until exhausted. Its power comes from elsewhere, but its will is its own.

3

No book is complete. Is it three times I have rewritten mine? At night, the sun gathers stars around, in the morning, the feathery creatures we remember.

When we read page after page of the sparkling stars of sleep, of the beating wings and flight of birds, do we not admit that writing too has that supreme power we grant above all to death, the power to transform the world, to justify the image of the universe in its many unknowable changes?

Wondrous course of death. Was I present at its start? Death celebrates death with pomp or restraint. Every departure is premeditated, every trespass guided by antennae. The spring joins the hand to the twelve marks on the dial. The key is in our hands. The figure clears the echo.

4

("It is cool in the shade, Reb Semihon. We might as well talk in the sun."

"It is not yet time, Reb Serna. We have only just started."

"It is cold where we are, Reb Semihon, and we are dressed lightly."

"Where the dialogue starts it is always cold, Reb Serna."

"The sun, Reb Semihon, will clear our minds and strengthen our bodies."

"We will soon be hot, Reb Serna. And the sun will be down.")

DRAWN CURTAINS

"Dullness of words where God speaks. A dark which feels good. Drawn curtains. On the dark page lines continue the crease and the dream, the space between."

—Reb Rissel

1

"Hope: the following page. Do not close the book."

"I have turned all the pages of the book without finding hope."

"Perhaps hope is the book."

2

"In my dialogues there are no answers. But sometimes a question is the flash of an answer.

"My route riddled with crystals."

—Reb Librad

And Yukel said:

"If an answer were possible death would not travel alongside life, life would not have a shadow. The universe would be light.

"Contradiction is the scream of a soul drawn and quartered by the moment. Did not Reb Sedra write: 'Here is grain for your field: a grain of life, a grain of death. The grain of life will nourish your death, the grain of death feed your life.'"

("Death will get the better of me. God can only help me in the void."

—Reb Zeilein)

THE LOOP

"One of my great fears," said Reb Aghim, "was to see my life round itself into a loop without being able to stop it."

Reb Ardash wrote: "To be in the truth means accepting ugliness on the same grounds as beauty. Religion is the region of the soul where truth is protected from itself. God plays against God for a reassuring image of His power. There is no divine Truth. There is a desire, a foolishness of God's which quickens in goodness where the circle is made certain."

"Blasphemy," replied Reb Séri. "God's Truth is the summer of the world, not its venom. It is the gold of the first morning. You only know the rue in truth. You suffer from truth-ache. Ah, may you get well."

And Reb Ardash said: "It is not always the heart which closes the loop. Sometimes it is the teeth. There are celestial bites which witness God's despair."

THE HOLE

("My love, if time had your voice you would be the call of the seasons. But you withdraw.
"My life: yesterday."

(Yukel's Notebook)

"Before old age, before the night when I am a shadow and hollow."

(Yukel's Notebook)

"The night so low our fingers can portion out the shadows."

(Yukel's Notebook)

"Seaweed will do to adorn a forehead."
—Reb Hati

"Why praise a tree fed by a river when it has bitter fruit?
"The world and its beings—rivers that cut to our hearts.
"I adjust."

—Reb Gueddah)

The book is a labyrinth. You think you are leaving and only get in deeper. You have no chance of running off. For that, you must destroy the work. You cannot make up your mind to do that. I notice your anxiety mounting. Slowly but surely. Wall after wall. Who awaits you at the end? Nobody. Who will leaf through you, decipher, love you? No doubt, nobody. You are alone in the night, alone in the world. Your solitude is the solitude of death. Another step. Somebody will perhaps come and pierce the wall, will find a way out for you. Alas. Nobody ventures here. The book bears your name. Your name clenched like a fist clenched on a sword.

Ridiculous, on your belly like this. Crawling. Drilling the wall at its base. Hoping to escape like a rat. Like the dark in the morning, on the road.

And this determination to stay upright in spite of being tired and hungry?

A hole, just a hole,

the chance of the book.

> "In the daytime you discover a thing, in the heart of night you see it."
>
> —Reb Monem

BEADS OF SWEAT

("The water was so confined in its course that sweat seemed to be a spring."
                                        —Reb Vétah

*"A voice wants a face
where we no longer see.
Heavy, moonless night."*
                                        (Yukel's Notebook)

*"You took your turn on the road of exile.
Ah, you were not alone. Therefore you walked alone."*
                                        —Reb Jessiah

*"Land I leave behind,
the salt of life
is in the memory
of which I will die.
Held by the deep
like an anchored ship.
Water—my agony."*

                                        —Reb Sécoth)

World of my works where thirst shimmers like beads of sweat on a tanned chest, will I be able to distract from the dawn the page to be written,
to be cooled with wary words better than water under a rock?
Death is sweet like the dark. Thirst makes do with its bed.
I write while night unfolds.
The invisible form of the book is the legible body of God.
In the fire, words are cinders.
False butterfly—death lodged in its probe.
I walk behind the wind, and the stifled scream of words is only a bit of dust under my feet.

Now the book is done. Three times the lesson of the book. Night is inside it forever.

I started out wanting to forget, and the void mapped my route. Nothing more certain: you cannot turn green again, away from your roots.

Dry branches of my felled trees. The forest counts on its excess of sap.

Faithful beyond horizons,

with passionate prow my vessel cleaves the ocean which a bird high in the air displaces.

Fluid, every flight,

water writhes, leaps, flows.

I watch the glance, which held you, die.

> *("Our colloquies were confident, in close touch with our relays. The road sucks us in and thus disappears. One shadow is enough for the night, one button of gold for the day. Ink shrinks space down to the letter. You will print the earth in its split attention. You will print the sky in its diffuse impossibility. Rectangles of grass or sand, or blue or clouds. The rays of the sun are penholders which night gorges with ink."*
>
> —Reb Adal)

The fate of the word is the fate of our passions. A writer questions himself forever in the infinite solitude of God whose gesture he has inherited, but with its fire gone out. Rekindling the divine gesture again and again, this is our contribution to the light.

We are at the heart of creation, absent from the All, in the marrow and moire of Absence, with the Void for recourse, for a means to be and to survive. So that, in the creative act, we are and even surpass the Void facing the restoring All.

Book rejected and reclaimed by the book. The word, for which I was pain and meditation, discovers that its true place is the non-place where God lives resplendent with not being, with never having been. Therefore interpretations of Elohim, approaches to Adonai can only be personal, laws only individual laws, truths only solitary truths in the scream they wrench from us. And this even within the possibility of transmitting a recognized Truth, a common and sealed law.

Instinct of the work, infallible flair. Did not Reb Gabriah compare his goose quill to a dog's muzzle?

The work imposes its choices on us. Only much later the writer becomes aware of this. Can he claim its daring if the choice is bold?

Death is of this world. It is on our planet that we will live death, along with plants and days.

Where I go, night overtakes me. It is Sarah and Yukel in their short lives. It is the dead hour at the bottom of the hour.

—Where I go

in their tears,

their hearts—

Ah, the sun will catch me, in my disturbing transparency.

What am I but an awareness of the dark, forever?

And yet

I am certain I exist in the crystal of writings whose luster I could keep in check if I wanted. The world is within me, and I exist through the world.

Did I know, when I let the first sentences of the book invade me, did I know that it would lead me from threshold to threshold to the summer of death?

The past takes part in its own metamorphoses for the sake of a future which eternity turns away from the perishable everyday.

You cannot build on ambiguity.

Only granite will do.

Paris feasts on its amazing past. The streets have pupils dim with dreams. The passersby mingle and separate like shadows of crazy birds.

Clear autumn morning. The sun probes the ground. And the air is russet. The story of Sarah and Yukel is on the lips of unhappy lovers. They smiled to have known the springtime of flesh and soul where one moment blossoms into another. They cried to have seen the storm lay waste the beach.

Ah, that caresses could reach under the skin, reach bones and blood.

Paris is white. Paris rejoins the old Paris in its whiteness. Its buildings again astound time.

Here, at the Carrefour de l'Odéon, I met Yukel five years ago. I had just left the house. I had hardly gone a few steps when he caught up with me. I do not remember which of us spoke first. We walked side by side. We were two breaths, two echoes. We seemed to continue a conversation long interrupted: our sentences, forged by distance, always submitted to an old order and registered at the far end of silence.

Who are these characters who have since replaced us with their claim to be heard? Did I unearth them from the book of sand?

Sarah is a grape on the road. Our sages lived in the land of the Dead Sea and of olives, in the kingdom of vulture and scorpion. They left us their songs and their sobs.

Scorpions stung Sarah's eyes, vultures ransacked her forehead while the bitter water and black fruit delivered her lover to death. A whole country hounded them.

Cruel Israel, yet prompt in your hospitality. Fatherland held up by our groans and hopes like a silver platter by a dutiful servant. The words of my book rest on your precious metal. Will you drink a round of them, pioneers and guests, scholars and prophets?

Cruel Israel, hapless fields which demand more than the arms and the back of a man can do,

but which the orange tree consoles,

we are the example and sternness of wounded courage whose stem checks the wind.

I will not stop at the port.

I will remain witness of the prophecy at the door of God's favorite spot on the globe.

I will remain silence and scream while the grain sways at the foot of your mountains in summer and the sand grows heavy with the visits of water.

I have told of the desert through the indestructible memory of the void whose every grain is a tiny mirror.

A stranger to my brothers,

a stranger to myself,

to the world
in the rigorous chance of the book.

> *("The sun," noted Reb Gabbar, "is a flaming hoop which a little girl trundles around the earth. Nobody has ever discovered the child even though she plays in broad daylight."*
>
> *"If you questioned a shadow it would most likely answer you with an arch of night, and you would have to face each new star."*
> —Reb Léres)

O death, questioning quest!

And Yukel said:

"This is the room. The bed, the table, the walls, the roof.
"Here lived Sarah.
"Here lived Yukel.
"There is as much reality in these two rooms, these two dwellings as in the street, the camps, the clinic where Sarah was taken.
"In the book reality learns and reveals what it is: a visible irreality which we confront with itself, with its base in the summoned word."

> *("If grass is the question of life sand is perhaps its answer. Then I would have devoted my life to pestering the desert."*
> —Reb Mitri)

This was the completion of the book: inserting the page with the three essential questions.
This was the book in the image of the world and the apple whose roundness has made me think that original sin was only an insane

quest for divine harmony. To be a world in a hand and a word. To say what is written, to create what is read.

This was the eternal beginning of the book in its conscious rigor and freedom where God is the Sign.

Educating your eyes is no pipe dream. I see ever farther, pushed by I do not know what need to understand and love, farther yet till I shall find myself back at my point of departure. What matter where I think I am going if any course inevitably returns to our origins. We never overtake our steps.

I am haunted by the memory I mentioned of a buffalo tied to her wheel to spread the bountiful water.

Have I given drink, I who know only thirst.

I, absent from myself,

I, Yukel Serafi, whose life and story are summed up in a few sentences?

I share the fate of the worn-out beast in its self-willed night.

Let my works be my three torches

and let my heart, which no longer beats in unison with my heroes', grow sober like theirs and freeze near the rendered page.

Man does not exist. God does not exist. The world alone exists through God and man in the open book.

Yaël
(1967)

. . . This dream: a dreadful smothering of the soul,
then a lofty idea of death, then an ordinary note pad
where the day butts against the night.

FORESPEECH

I say: I am death, and forthwith am before God was.
If we spurn God's image, do we not reject creation?
Then where is truth but in the burning space be-
tween one letter and the next?
Thus the book is first read outside its limits.

1

*(God is the measured and immeasurable death of
God.*

*He who has destroyed himself: what can he remem-
ber but notorious destructions?*

*Scream: desire of the book before the book, O
death, with you all has been said.*

*Vital knot—why do I think of vipers' knot? A burst
of sun and sea has struck the universe with liquid fire.*
*Does a word not die as surely of the colored poison
of the pen as by a pointed stone or knife? Once finished
off in its standard form, it is read, it is born.*
*Thus we see the beginning through Good and Evil,
the embodiment of our short-lived laws.*
*Our birth enters the immemorial moment of the
death of God and the world.)*

He who cheated you out of your world by some trick or other
deserves only violent hatred. Against the Enemy of the soul the battle must be decisive.
If you win you will later (no doubt because you are lonely and

tired) be indulgent with your victim, and someday, who knows, even tender. But beware of the senseless love which leads to desiring God with a passion.

He who pretends to give all deprives us of our future. Giving means opening out, means forging our tomorrows from the best in us gathered for others. God hampers universal brotherhood. He forbids man to imagine kindness.

But for those who are in love with the absolute, obsessed by eternity, turning to God to adore or destroy Him means reaching the depth of human anguish. For we are desperately driven to claim responsibility for the death of God in order to love Him more than ourselves, against ourselves.

A great love carries within it a mourning for love.

O Yaël, how I would have loved you in my misery.

2

(The word is a test, the summons a pact.

Dawn. And the end of the day. Eternity is preserved.)

3

With nothing left to invent, God drowned in Himself. It would be interesting to know which was His last invention—the fatal one. Some claim it was man.

(Innocence of Evil. Could it be that original sin was, rather than a sin of knowledge, the part we played in the death of God which, for being born last, we take entirely upon ourselves?)

4

*(Have I, in my hope to undo the evil that eats us,
held your head too long under water? Your child's-
head, lissom dawn and sponge?*

*Shore of absence where the body ran aground, the
light, free of bandied words, spreads from mouth to
ear for you, O living-dead.*

*You, half open at the core. In your flesh I violate
the void.)*

A circle
and in the circle another
circle
and in the new circle still
another circle
and so on till
the last: a forceful
point,
then an invisible point
unbelievably present,
majestically absent.
A woman and a word.
A woman turning
around a word turning
slowly, faster,
unbelievably fast
till they are but
one circle in the space that spawned them
pursuing a smaller
and even smaller,
   ntesquely tiny circle.
A hole. An empty socket.
An eye of night.
A shattered eyeball.
And then? You look.

You plunge.
Is this what is called unity:
a circle undone?
A circular scream,
step,
and avowal?

5

> *(Was it perhaps your heart, Yaël, that made me*
> *hate God?*
>
> *I took you in as a word.*
>
> *"I" is the book.)*

On the 17th of March, last year, I had a dream which left me very
upset.
A woman used my life for her own ends.
"Lilith, Eve, Cressida? Which one?" Gabriel will write me later.
"The lie of God," I said to myself.
"Beautiful through death.
"No doubt ours."

6

> *(One man suggests that Eve was God's first word*
> *of love; another, on the contrary, that she was His last.*
> *Eve betrayed God*
> *and God created night.*
>
> *We shall seize the pathos of the lie in all its brutal-*
> *ity.*
> *O voice of rose and mud.*
>
> *Is it in the end a matter of finding out if perhaps*

speech was given to us only so that we could settle down in the lie?

Luckily we die of it. And against us, at the cost of our flesh and blood, truth stamps itself in glittering negative letters

> *on the blue void,*
> *on the black nothing.*

Listen: in every vowel and every consonant beats the pulse of the book, blankly oblivious of the world.)

THE LIGHT OF THE SEA

If you burn a book, it opens unto absence in the flame. If you drown it, it unfolds with the wave. If you bury it, it quenches the thirst of the desert. Because all words are pure water of salvation.

With a tree on fire the earth matches a sky full of fruit.

If we want to cross the threshold of truth we must cease to be, in the midst of what is.

Man and nature trade shadow and life.

The universe of shadows is the universe of an eye swept away in a flood. Night's consciousness: a dead star.

Absent, the creature perceives the infinite.

On the level of creation, the pupils are giant breasts. The world is an infant to whom the eyes give suck.

At no time was the building an obstacle.
The stones are of passion,
the portal of reason.

Avoid confusing face and features. The face is omen, the features are attributes.

Tern, swallow of the sea. The ocean has its own springtime.

The book, I have to admit, is closer to an anthology than to an epic.

The light of the sea adapts to the angry as well as to the cheerful wave. It has its string of dreams and its salt tears. This central brightness which envelops the world to the point of hiding it, in the daytime, from man, is it not the space beyond the page where our frustrated thoughts move, poor worlds led astray?

If we no longer think, it does not mean we stop thinking. Thought is the conscious and unconscious of the world. When a musician stops playing on his instrument it does not mean he no longer hears the sounds of the work he played. The brain takes the place of the ear. Memory revives with each note that is found again.

Have I lived in my memory? Is this how I remember so precisely a slice of vagabond life which I can hardly believe I lived? *The other*'s life, yet mine in Yaël's wake whose face changed so constantly that every instant claimed it as its own. Thus our memories give us back our words, and we question the signs they gather for us to meditate on. Facing an accomplished fact we push our self-questioning through writing to the dimmest borders of the being that escapes us. We die a death for two where the book is born.

In the book, order is primeval whereas disorder is the systematic refusal to complete the work which every page reinforces with its void.

Making a book or, rather, helping it to come into being means above all blurring its utopian tracks, wiping out footprints. Then the word takes the place still warm from the heel. And we go to the word and with it retrace our silent, forgotten way, a way taken for and without it.

The book commands, and we guide the book. A writer's life is a steady march toward a star. The constellations answer for his work. Black stars, which recall night, lined up for what festivities? On the page they no longer shine for the eye but for the mind.

"My eyes will be my thoughts, and my hands my road," said the stranger whose voice sounds like mine when I create.

Improvised paths of the eyes: a shadow mourns for a thing. Once its preeminence is expressed, appearance rejects appearance.

In the name of His creatures God accepts the world of a foreboding glimmer which like a gold dot blinking in space reveals in flashes (O moving solitude) the imperceptible broken line of death.

THE STORY

In the morning of flesh, death joins the death of the world.

Thus the sap assents to the sapwood.

God is the death of man, and man a moment in the graven death of God.

Ringing song of men. Campanula, the bluebell, will be my flower.

God
or the thunder that was His voice,
or the lightning that was His gesture,
or the delicate cloud He once was,
or the sky, air, water that together are His
    absence,
or fire which is pain.
our pain, Yaël,
our real and great pain.

O death, your eyes will be mine, and my freedom that of the prow.

Rice fields of the night. At dawn, tireless women with naked arms and thighs fill their baskets with stars.

Factual truth means only that others (and we ourselves) accept our interpretation of an event.

The samphire is the queen of rocks. Passion dislodges stones.

Yaël's Death

O Yaël, proscribed word.

Her first name intrigued me from the moment I heard it.

Sun of Nuriel and Uriel, master of Tahariel, Padaël, Raziel. It also reminded me of Jofiel, Zagzaguel, Achatriel, Raphaël. But it was a woman who bore it, and I realized I would love Yaël in the lips of the black crater of her name.

Countenance of God, O infinite effacing of the Face.

I remember she had her hair down that morning so that it covered her back. Black hair with a soft blue shimmer. My hand passed through it, now like a sturgeon, now like a starfish.

She was lying down. I had lifted her head with one hand, and this hand was life and its five roads, and her head was the globe.

The middle road is the hardest to follow. The longest in time. Road of noon or midnight, both day and night have set and colored it.

Was I going to explore the world by taking all its roads? But were these roads? At most, signs that people had passed this way. And even at that I was not sure they could be trusted.

Her nightgown (as if dawn were always wandering over her body) kept me from touching her. I stroked her breasts, but they were veiled breasts; I stroked her belly, but it was a veiled belly. Except for her face, only her neck and shoulders were of flesh. And her arms.

She did not react. Was she already dead or half-dead, engulfed? Heavy in the water, covered with algae, between two waves near the shore?

I was determined to save her. There was not a minute to lose. I would lay her down on the sand and make her breathe again.

I remember that morning, at dawn—or was it another morning just as grey, elsewhere, in another room?

> (. . . *in the void perhaps, land of strange souls, or elsewhere, as in a dream, in a land so far from mine that I do not know its name, and yet so attractive. Voluptuous female body the size of a continent, land like a nape or a breast with borders of down, pale land between two rings like those under the eyes of lovers which betray an infinite longing for the dark. . . ?*)

That morning—we often stayed up late after dinner, at home, or with friends in some bar—that morning or that night, I do not remember which, when she had drawn the curtains, undressed, and put out the chandelier for the dimmer bedside lamp, I lay down beside her in bed. She did not budge, braced in her refusal.

There was a gentle plush or felt animal in a corner. You could not say for sure if it moved or lay still, but you could clearly hear it breathing. It seemed a wounded beast whose breath was closer to a rattle and near whom you could have found traces of blood.

Frozen in the rim, in the edge of light outlined in the mirror, cheek against cheek, temple against temple, we could have been taken for the image of what rare coin or ivory medallion in its padded frame ready to be nailed to the wall: the effigy of the Monarch and Queen, of the conqueror and his favorite.

Was it me or *the other* embracing her? *The other*, no doubt, whom Yaël always spoke to, always looked at with so much kindness that it hurt me deeply. However, that morning or that night, I do not remember which, something strange happened which I cannot get out of my mind. I was no longer the same. I was no longer myself. I was *the other* or, rather, I finally took his place and was so excited, so grateful to the auspicious hour and the whole world that I lost control and pressed Yaël to myself so long that she collapsed without a sign of life.

I plunged into her eyes now without limits. I prayed for the moment when her lids would close and I would stop rolling through the void. I felt light, but condemned beyond remedy. I would kill myself soon, at the end of the night, and it would be the brutal end of a being who had never known why he lived.

Yet, without being absolutely sure, I think I remember being not worried only about myself. I was anxious about Yaël's death more than about my own.

My soul was stricken with remorse, bruised.

How did I manage to seize Yaël's wrist? I found myself in the bedroom, my arm against the sheet. I convinced myself that her pulse was still beating. Her life gave me back my life just as her death had hurled me toward my own.

I remember I closely examined my hands before questioning them as the Officer would do once he arrived with his "What do you have to say for yourself?"—but of course I did not do it as efficiently because I do not know the police methods of investigation.

I would say—but would I defend myself? I did not feel the need—I would say: "Yaël . . ." as if I were still speaking to her, but for the last time. I would say: "I would have liked to help you, Yaël, because that way I would have acted in keeping with my soul. I do not know if I killed you or if you died on the threshold of an impossible love, on the margins of my death." The Officer would refuse to let me get off this easily, and he would be right. But do I know what happened that night or that morning? I do not remember.

There was Yaël in bed and I beside her. I had taken her face in my hands, and her eyes were so hard, so cruelly, so stubbornly hard that the few words I heard seemed to be pronounced by her pupils.

I put out the lamp. It was light in the room. Had I pushed open the shutters to let a ray of moon in? The dark lifted at the borders of a whiter dark. But perhaps it was really morning and we were still asleep, morning welcomed through the lids of a lazy awakening, lids so thin, so nearly transparent that we kept them half-closed in order to savor the soft fore-light, the freshness of a rosy dark.

Propped on my elbow, I looked at Yaël. My face above hers was the corner stone of a crumbling wall, the eye of a storm like the center of a celestial wound which plunged the world into terror. She screamed. Getting away from me, keeping me at a distance with all the strength of her stretched arms, was her way of escaping destruction and death. Under the weight of my chest her arms gave, little by little. Then there was nothing to keep us apart but the moisture of our bodies in their untidy nakedness.

I was no longer *the other*. He stood behind me. I realized that the immense distance Yaël had tried to put between us canceled the apparent distance between *the other* and me, so that I was the nightmare she fought by clutching her lover across my hands which did not let go of her neck. Her eyes told him her love, told him her repulsion for me. They told him her faithfulness beyond death.

I turned. I was alone. With silence for an accomplice. Yaël's screams hung on the ceiling like game hung up by their legs. The sky had been pulled down with those poor beasts.

The Book

If there were no more earth or sky there would still be us in the naked years we keep.

You never lose the book: you lose yourself.

I have not left my apartment. What day is it? It hardly matters. I have reread the pages written after my crime. I reread my journal as well as some sheets I had kept (since when?) in the same box. Mechanically I put them in order on top of the story of my crime and of my journal. Thus I gave birth to the book which I had composed without noticing. I mean without actually thinking of it in the course of these months outside the book.

The book does not need man to come into being. It does so through him. As in our lives we are forever pushed by the hours, one after the other. A book which could have held all the words for our thoughts and gestures, but which definitely kept only those it chose to make common cause with in their order and economy.

No way, therefore, to develop certain sentences, to add others which might have turned them from the tendency toward aphorism they so often give in to. They refused, strengthened in their attitude by a lofty idea of the book within the book, as if their concision, their proud contraction housed the light which lights up the work from within.

The book had the ambition to be the book of the eyes.

Beings and things exist only in the mirrors which copy them. We are countless crystal facets where the world is reflected and drives us back to our own reflections, so that we can know ourselves only through the universe and what little it retains of us.

The knowledge we have of ourselves rests on the interpretation of an earlier interpretation which we confirm on awaking and which precedes us into death whose instant will relate our stages across the nights.

Were the eight months before my crime only months of writing? And what is the mystery of this book which I have led to its conclusion at the price of the life of an imaginary being who was my reason to live? But is it only these eight months of pain and anxiety? Was this book not conceived earlier, much earlier? In that case everything had to happen as it did for the book. In that case I have been the instrument of an inexorable fate which the words made me take on myself.

I think of the book, and Yaël is no more. Did she die before she was born like the child of her first love? Then she and I never left the invisible kingdom of the dead where we got lost thinking we were going our ways, I in search of her, she in her desire for *the other*.

What does it matter now if she was murdered or not? Death does not have the sense we give it in death. A violent death is tied to the healthiest and worthiest act of truth. It is a dawn which all the scattered and lost shadows come to salute with a red gesture faithful to fire.

"You are a storyteller," a friend said to me one day.

How can I be when words and images always cut in and want to be heard with their own aura, when the story is built out of bits of counter-stories, and when silence lies in wait for the world?

Elya
(1969)

In back of the book there is the ground of the book. In back of the ground there is immense space and, hidden in this immense space, the book we are going to write in its enigmatic sequence.

Everything is before Everything. The word is the day after the word, and the book the day after the book.

So that we turn forever around what was and will be and which, in the image of God's proud absence, stays what is, namely: the mysterious tie to the universe and the place where this universe waits to be discovered.

Let us perforate oblivion. Because oblivion is the thick rind around our origins.

The initial sin is a sin of memory. We will never get to the end of time.

I will end up with nothing saved out of this attempt to pull free of the yoke of words, attempt which, one day, got stuck in its own swamp.

The book belongs to the book.

Elya, it was written that we would rejoin you where we had thought we were leading you.

There is no help against this night.

A PUDDLE OF WATER

("The book," I was told by a sage I sincerely respect, "contains a face which we wrinkle in writing.
"The older the book the purer the face."

And he added: "Do not believe that the book [which is not spared illness] disappears with the book. It dies only in its filigree. We know it is up to us to look for it beyond where it will give us back our written world."

He said further: "A lake is at the peak of power because it is a master over the reflections which haunt it. Likewise the book when it lets us hear and drink.")

Rain had left a puddle in the street, several inches deep, which the mud made into a lake buried in its misery.

However, the sun played there at inventing colors and getting them to correspond.

I was watching this unexpected concert of reflections when, suddenly, a car turned the corner, barreled across the puddle and splashed me.

Is the book, in its beginning, a puddle like this whose music enchanted me for a minute or, rather, the muck on my flannel pants like flakes of a wilted page where writing was tackled?

I was waiting for Yaël.—Why, in fact, was I waiting for her when she was dead?—Paris, moreover, had been basking in a radiant sun for a whole week.

This puddle is maybe Elya, a forbidden brew, Elya as you might imagine him, not knowing his life. But his life, threatened all the short while it lasted, had it not had the face of an eternal child bend over it so closely as to take on its features?

We have not done fighting when we die. The seasons bathe in rotting water as in the short-lived rainbow beginning to fade. They burn out in what was their reason to be.

When we met, Yaël, we had arrived, though still young, at the
end of our wandering: you becoming a word, and I, parallel, a man
of the Letter.

Nothing, however, let us know our time was so measured we
could no longer retrace our steps.

Face to face, accomplices, hangmen, victims of a silence of dream
and flesh which you had nourished in your soul and guts and which,
little by little, had become our only resort, our only chance of lib-
eration.

Cherished in his absence, this natural son of Nothing was going
to take everything from us. He appropriated (without a fair fight) the
book in the name of a truth which excluded us, you because of me,
and me through you. A truth to which we would return with our
regrets, our memories, and this need to survive which makes us in-
sist insolently at the threshold.

Cursed in our consciousness of speaking and in our heedless pre-
tention to succeed in it.

Our route is that of the great sinners for whom God is a dawn
secret without ties and which bleeds.

MEMORY OF A DEAD MEMORY

Death left you your chance: a deadly season without
fruit.

The sea assimilates us to the wave. Up to us to surge
and wear down the rock.

After death, the sea takes our measure.

Time searched through the past and made inseparable faces
march by for us, ours among them. But Elya's was lacking.

You could not suppress a gesture of irritation, Yaël, and you said
to me:

"My memories will supplement those of the days. I have never
lived within time."

(" . . . possibly dead"
—is how you described life close to our steps.)

After *Yaël, Elya*. After the word in ambush for the book, a book
of the refused word.

And as if autumn was only the falling of summer, and spring but
the fable of winter run down.

Nothingness is our All. The sky is a repeat of its own absence on
which the void bestows a relief of disintegrated constellations.

So that there is nothing at the beginning, nothing at the end but
a procedure caught in its hesitations and turns.

The beginning of the book is a beginning for being and things.

All writing invites to an anterior reading of the world which the
word urges and which we pursue to the limits of faded memory.

We can only write what we have been able to read. It is an infin-itesimal part of the universe to be told.

The book never actually surrenders.

> *("I imagine a writer who cannot reread himself."*
> *"Imagine. Imagine."*
> *"I imagine a book which cannot be abridged."*
> *"Imagine. Imagine."*
> *"I imagine a word become night, become all nights."*
> *"To this word we were prey.")*

Speaking of the book, Yaël said:

"The word would have to revive before we could approach its life tied to ours with every syllable.

"But on what page, in what plausible space conquered outside time?"

And she added:

"What we take for a written page is only a wager, on the level of the letter, to appropriate man and the world—which could only be done on the morning of death."

On the threshold of a rejected birth we write in the shadow of what has been written, but never read.

The book veils itself in the book.

As God does in God.

FROM DAY TO THE SHADOW OF DAY

1

The book is the place where a writer offers his voice up to silence.

Hence every margin is the beach of an avowal held back. And on its edge, the words gather and seal their alliance with the sea.

My bible is the page you cannot choose.

2

What can a stone reply to the charge that it is hard except that it is hard to last?

Tell me which road you take, and I will tell you who you will become, whom you will join.

1

All is created. You remember nothing. You see all.

One day, I learned my name from my books. You were not with me. I broke into the world which was going to be ours. The road stretched before me, split the horizon.

Nothing subsists in death, so memory is queen.

One day, I saw myself in all the stages I had gone through. My memories had gorged on memories down through the centuries.

So that I cannot tell in what era, on which continent I was born.

"The road taken by a Jew," some sage said, "is the imperceptible course of a drop of water from the mountaintop to the sea."

I will have been a Jew in my course.

> *(No roll of parchment holds a sentence of mine co-pied by hand. I write on the flimsiest, least durable material which perfectly suits the words relieved of my death.)*

So I will have been a Jew in the legitimate lightness of my pen.

God, in the book, can stand only God.

This Judaism after God, my kind, is a lake over which my questions hover like mountaintops, some of them out of reach. The lake has given birth to the river on which I have traveled without paying too much attention to the landscape, subdued by the absolute in motion which would flood me with the day.

Even the most daring diver could not separate the words in my books from the sentences written in the vast bottom of the sea where any question dies of its questioning.

The same death indefinitely opts for the same man.

My work bears witness to this as if from the extreme point of my being, at the dawn of all end and all birth.

I will have been a Jew for not being able to answer to any but myself, more of a stranger than anyone else, and close to the poorest in the losing word.

> *(. . . of a certain Judaism which takes its force and features from the word and is contemporary with the book.*
>
> *Deprived of God in His equivocal death where the creature's fate is a baroque pattern of writing.*
>
> *"O my lover," cried Yaël, "who was ever closer to*

the word than you who came to love it when it was
gently silent?")

2

Jew, for you the homeless fruit of aggressive silence.

So, with God dead, I found my Jewishness confirmed in the book,
at the predestined spot where it came upon its face, the saddest,
most unconsoled that man can have.

Because being Jewish means exiling yourself in the word and, at
the same time, weeping for your exile.

The return to the book is a return to forgotten sites.

God's heritage could only be handed on in the death He ushered
in.

At the end of our lives, with all tasks done, we will in turn hold
up the book of our apprenticeship.

(Circular work; you must tackle my work in its cir-
cles.

And each of them will demand a new reading.)

3

The day's freedom consists in the light's secret
climb back to the beginnings of the shores deserted by
men.

The heart beats in the emptiness of the astonished
body. Its form will come from *the other*.

COUNTER-TEST

With its stars of ink the book is a universe in motion which our eyes fix.

People of the Book, we will never have a house. We shall die in words.

Interpretation is bound to act on the fate of individuals and of the world. It gives their destiny a new course, taking full responsibility for it, being ready to suffer the consequences and pay the price.

Also, interpreting the Book means first of all rising up against God to take voice and pen out of His power. We have to get rid of the divine within us in order to give God back to Himself and fully enjoy our freedom as men.

Simplicity is the wisdom of summits.

From the outset it has been my own story unrolling before my eyes.

It cannot be yours because of course our routes differ, even though we share night as the womb from which we were one morning ejected.

All coincidence is leaven for existence against its dark finality. We moved the same milestones, but never knew where we were.

Riveted to space, to the place reserved for dreamers, we rest, delicate starfish, on the very bottom of the soul.

To accept life means proposing an explanation of existence. But which one could we adopt? They are all contradictory.

Purity of being at the two poles of innocence.

We intuit life only in its flight. Tomorrow will be another moment of the source.

Alliance of slack time and time woven. We shall never read the pages rejected from the book.

The space of a spark prolonged. Mock amazement.
You will not find God where He expects you, but where you expect the dawn.

You make awkward steps towards God—you run towards Nothing.

Divided, I will be innocently human, as opposed to God, wise and indivisible.

Not-knowing has knowing as its esplanade where God disclaims competence.

My hands are full when you give me your hand.
A feather of spray will never fly out of the well.

Night outside. Inside, lack of air, the flame consumed.
What darkness always weighs on the unsubdued paths of the soul.
Truth has no place. It is a glimmer of unlivable places.

You only sleep with one hand. The other spangles your sleep.
Skylights, skylights . . .

I aim to be, someday, seen.

What remains to be thought (the fruit) follows what has been thought (the tree). But there is something else unthought which is the irreducible desert where our steps are weighed down with the day.

Entering into God's thought means thinking the unthought.

Could divine presence, as glimpsed by the mind, be thought at the heart of the unthought infinite?—But all thinking rids us of God.

One writes before or after God.
God is the blank present.

DOOR II

Non-writing vies to spread from oblivion to death. The word will come in time to teach it.

Starting from oblivion, I carved a path which death was in favor of. I took the lesson of the second commandment literally. I abolished the world in the word to come. You were dead, Yaël. With you gone, I could advance where you had led and then left me. It was my chance to force the book to close and, reconciling word and step, to glimpse my dead name, your name, Yaël, with its innumerable dry branches.

You talked, devoured by the word kicking in your womb. And your speech was as if beheaded at its birth. What will be built is what was torn from you, easily or with effort.

Ah, how many times did you die for the Book? Killing you, I identified with each of its pages, I appropriated Elya.

> *(Keystone of the vault, key of the void,*
> *Elya: finally the key?*
>
> *After-night of the act. Behind us the night intact.)*

If we never knew who we were, Yaël, it was because we had forgotten. On the other side of the wall stretches the domain of oblivion. We knocked down the obstacle. A past we canceled struggles in our abandoned writings.

The book is always recognition of the book.

(We turned around the abyss, Yaël.
The abyss was your child.)

Hence a stillborn child. Stillborn, that is to say: dead in order to be born. Life refused even at its birth and stiff at this moment whose breath and inertia were ours.

Hence a sadistic truth which you gave the manifold face of your love. I would have been your son without being so, to the point of drowning in his night in turn. I would have been your lover without being so, to the point of dying in his skin.

This way we completed the cycle of death, O word to which I have given hope by throwing it into the chasm. Falling, the flower perfumes space. On such a persistent scent we will have built our last dwelling: not a tomb, but the book.

Thus, you could say, on a page-size barry field, there lined up a secret embryogeny with a bend for words (wing, appendix, bract, calyx, spur, sepal) which we seized and hastened to destroy. Probably from fear of being read in the unbearable bloom of our sedentary wanderings.

Once and for all, did we not ransack the garden?

The book really is fire under the axe.

Oblivion, fearful flower plucked at the hour of heaviest sleep. The bonded screams of the earth mingle with ours when dawn quickens its colors, when the corolla rivals the solar disk in short-lived beauty.

Any flower has the worth of oblivion.

Equivalence of rites.

Any flower has the warmth of oblivion.

PLEDGE OF THE ABYSS

1

(God gives death the dimensions of His absence.)

2

(To write as if addressing God. But what to expect from nothingness where any word is disarmed?

There is no far-off death.

Anchored in the night like one single diamond.

"What is memory?"
"A marvelous flight where all is black,
"a beautiful, luminous bird, soon to be black too."

Being means questioning. Means interrogating yourself in the labyrinths of the Question put to others and to God, and which does not expect any answer.

Night of mystery, total night.
Dawn will be a shock.

Night is the last to speak to absence.

Only what disappears will have called for us.

What did you hope for, what, if not to die the death of the lips in the word voted in.

If ever you should judge my book pernicious you

could, according to rabbinical recommendation, burn one half and bury the other.

But it will nonetheless stay written in space, as if each of its syllables were lit up by day or kindled by the dark in order to die of the dawn and rebound from a star.

All I know has come to me from reading the book, from its omens of nakedness, its nightly legibility.

The man who questions takes part in a universal interrogation with an abyss at its center. The book's configuration allows for this: it is the last circle of softened words.

No doubt your God needed a name in upper case to be struck honorably high.

Name too large for my mouth, will I never pronounce you? You are spared by your illicit absence.

"If You are able to punish, O Lord," said an insane mystic, "You should be able to punish Yourself.

"At the sight of evil whose very idea I cannot bear, do no longer veil Your face, but bruise Yourself without mercy.

"I shall be washed in Your guilty blood."

Vulnerable through whatever lays me open or smothers me, like the night, like the morning.

When it is time to leave the book I go back to it, as if from the pit of my resolution there emerged an irresistible command of the besieged page to reconsider it.

Thus we go into the death our feet had unwittingly trod on.

Through such repeated renewals, in night's slow rhythm, the light reaches the day.

Hope is bound to writing. And what greater hope than that of the feverish, hungry man for whom reading and adventures are selective seeds?

In my search for origins I have never really known which roads I took. They are so varied, so many.
Any beginning ends when it is marked.
The exordium finds its conclusion in tomorrow's stubborn silence.

We were walking along the Seine, Yaël. I remember it well. Near the Pont-Neuf, some weeks before my crime.

You suddenly said to me: "My stillborn child was in the image of the world. God's life is a life surrounded by emptiness. We daily watch how the forbidden flora of universal death, which precedes our own, blossoms on our banks."

The glory of the book is posthumous.

Aely
(1972)

THE THRESHOLD OF THE EYE

Within the word *oeil*, "eye," there is the word *loi*, "law." Every look contains the law.

A book—and dying words entertain you with the immortality of the Creator and created.

"God is the future of death," he said. "However, future means life.

"I imagine a body so inviolable that it would last forever, but death wastes the body first. Does waste take the place of the future? This would mean that God reproduces Himself out of His sacrificial Totality, that is, out of the boldness of Nothing. Schizogenetic void which braves the void in the name of an emptiness as dizzying as the universe and which is, if not God, at least His immortality."

"God's absence is immortal," he had jotted down one day, "and God only the reference to this immortality."

THE THRESHOLD OF THE VOID

. . . perhaps the unproven certainty of a law, a merciless law,

the law of Good in the swamps of Evil.

The book is not built, but unbuilt. God dies of the book.

The book, bottomless tomb of God?

This unbuilding means a return to the initial word.

Basic law of the space before night, both dark and light scatter its principle to the winds.

An architect's blueprint shows through the white sheet.

The writer builds his house in the invisible and immediately destroys it so it can be everybody's house forever.

Does the dark let us read the stars, and the splayed light the roots? Then the law of the book is the law of the infinite, law of what has always been empty, law of hospitality and silence.

The route of writing goes through the night. Will other eyes see for us where we can no longer see? We are never lost.

"It is uncontrovertible," he said, "that summer is the eye of the seasons."

"It is doubtful," he also said, "that the star sees the pebble, but, on the other hand, certain that the pebble sees the star."

(The dark, which God burdened with His creation, is again blank on awakening.

In the morning, you tear up the pages of your fever,

but every word naturally leads you back to its color,
its night.

Morning counts its dead, enumerates the lined-up
words of our differences.
Day is edged with mourning.

"God," he said, "is the harrowing reply to the post-
humous accusations of Creation."

"If you bend over your page," he said, "and do not
suddenly tremble with fear, throw away your pen.
Your writing would have little value.")

"I am not called Aely. Nobody has given me this name. It is the
name of a book. Am I this book? I can only be so in so far as it is the
deciphered silence of a name,

"so that we support each other in similar and pathetic absence.

". . . But this absence cannot be evoked.

"I have no life and never had one.

"I do not exist.

"I escape all that escapes me, escapes you,

"you who talk,

"who pursue me,

"who die."

Voice from the far side of silence, ah, how clear it was here.

("Aely," I repeated, "Aely, the elsewhere of an un-
imaginable elsewhere,
  seed of silence."

Dreaming is above us, silence below, in stones.

"Sky, earth, and sea are contained in stone," he
said, "and on the scales of the universal balance, it is
the measuring unit of silence.")

THE BOOK BELONGS ONLY TO THE BOOK

("I have no blood but has been shed," he said, "no ink but has been claimed by the words among which I ventured until, O transliteration of the dark sign into letters of bone, I was only the beginning of a written death which the words let me share.

"Invisible door. All houses are restored to the air. Did you know that emptiness is a sequence of doors lit by yesterday's light?"

"What is this place?" he continued to note. "A nest at the bottom of which a bird has buried a portion of eternity saved by its wings.

"Word, you were at least once a bird of prey, a bird of night. Dawn found you dead. The page is the implacable day.")

THE BOOK

The dark has the light for its past, and light the dark.

Whichever path we take, the past sputters in the distance like the last bit of a wick.

We find the candle where we left it for the time of a reading.

The book is the place of these far-flung comings and goings.

. . . from night to night, from this side of the past to the other.

The work I write immediately rewrites itself in the book.

This repeatability is part of its own breathing and of the reduplication of each of its signs.

If inspiration consists in filling your lungs with oxygen, expiration empties them of life, means gliding into the void.

Thus we only hold on to the world by agreeing, in advance, to die.

"The difficulty of writing," he said, "is only the difficulty of breathing in rhythm with the book."

"The book," he added, "is not a place, but a covert."

The word is dry at its death.

"Was it not a mouth propped open, round, which

inspired the mathematician to designate the void by a circle with an oblique bar?"

Leave me suspended in my life where nothing turns solid. Completion is the kiss of death.

Aely unfolds in time with silence spreading its wings.

He branches out beyond existence. Beyond you, Yaël. In Elya's wake.

. . . His body, I thought, belongs to someone else, some other night.

. . . Life without word or act, without wound or coupling, without listening or pardon.

To any life-beyond corresponds a death-beyond. This second life and anachronistic death are sisters.

(Shadow of a child of shadows: Aely.

And I said to myself that this shadow was perhaps always fused with that of Yaël cradling Elya in her arms and, later, with that of Elya without Yaël.

Aely is the way death will escape me as life did. Elusive down to his name which we never know how to pronounce. He is what does not go out from or come to me. He is the apocalyptic void which fascinates me from afar, which I can neither approach nor appreciate, which presents itself as the very last moment of death, moment when a name passes into its absence, which I will one day be called to take on by no longer taking myself on.

Between these two deaths, at the heart of these two deaths, breathes and no longer breathes the world.

Hence there could be a dark among all dark, a road among all roads, a line among all curved or straight lines. And we do not even need to know it. Behind us, above; before us, underneath: we shall be spotted in our death by a death which nobody could pay attention to and which will never ask anything of us; a death which calls into question everything down to the fundamental principle of all existence, scoffing at it because we sense its incompleteness, offering its own mystery instead; a death which grabs our last chance to restore it to itself as the dark gives the light back to the light; a death forgotten by death, insensitive to either idea or form and ruling a smooth universe. Then nothing has any sense. The question "Who are we?" is superfluous. Nothing concerns us any more, nothing, nothing, nothing . . .)

It is in the vague space of an anticipated word that Aely would watch us.

Who could have foreseen that silence is so patient? O night.

The world leaves us in peace unless we indulge in confidences.

There is that which finishes us off and then finishes off what, even finished, still contains a particle of us.

There is a finish coincident with any finishing, but which resists it in order to finish it off in its future.

Aely, power of the farthest distance.

. . . power of farthest distance and of what has not been thought.

Could it be that the void resets our name backwards?

Listen to time breathing. Eternity's breath is imperceptible.

El or the Last Book

•

(1973)

To blind all eyes for the glory of one.

What is this interpenetration and mutual engendering of the eye and the law but desire revealing its disconcerting tendencies and strength where, henceforward, nothing is left to be desired.

Eye rises up against eye. Through its victory over an enemy mortally wounded, we are called to see.

The victorious eye trumpets its truth. The vanquished eye takes refuge in its defeat. The book escapes both.

Rose death, morose meditation of the setting sun. The head of the captured dragon about to be cut off will roll into the dark abyss of worlds. Waking. Sleep. Reawakening. Revolutions. O dream, evolutions. The end is always in the next word.

Striations in rock from the sliding glaciers of an earlier age or barely perceptible lines on the surface of some crystals: between their scars, the law penetrates everywhere and rules on the authority of an unsuspected death preceding ours.

> You said: "Love is death's crystal day, oblivion its opaque night."

> "How beautiful you are, Sarah, lying here, naked, while I looked for you wherever you are not, where you no longer are," wrote Yukel.

> " . . . écrit, récit, the 'written' and the 'tale': one and the same word with its letters scrambled in a most natural way.
> "All writing offers its share of the telling," she said.

> No roots. Grow roots.

*There is no path but leads to our death, the path
we would prefer not to take.*

"How can I be both where I am dying and where
there is no love but in life?" *he had scribbled in his
notebook.*

"The sage dipped his reed pen into the inkwell,
pulled it out, and held it for a few moments, as if in
doubt, above the page where he had not yet noted anything that day. Then, to his pupil's surprise, he drew
a small circle in a corner of the blotter he always kept
within reach.

"'This circle,' he said, 'which the blotter has made
into a point invaded by night, is God.'

"'Why did you want the circle to turn into a black
point? And why should this stain among so many others on your blotter be God?' the disciple asked.

"'Your question is that of the Lord,' replied the
sage.

"'If my question is that of the Lord,' said the disciple, 'I know now that God has created me in His image.'"

Is it to this passage from Elya, *this reflection from
long ago, that the following pages owe their existence?
All my books have come about in this way. Some ob-
servation, often banal, some breach, some fear, anxiety or pain have in turn prepared their birth.*

*Here, yesterday's circle has shrunk to a point, the
questioning of the circle to that of the point.*

*Out of the nothingness of the book, a deeper noth-
ing strove towards light, conniving with a rebel point
which the infinite dark had hidden from me.*

"An accident," *he said,* "may suddenly transform
the infinite into infinite worlds whose interrelation we
cannot define, but which we nevertheless sense."

The point, an accident? Day, an accident?

*Then this book, like the preceding ones, is the fruit
of an accident.*

A wound is a shared frontier. The time of the infinite is the time of borders crossed.

No trace of blood remains where I have passed. What could be more natural? Only absence has the power to endure, but its oblivion shapes the negative into a dazzling point, a sun beyond alliance, beyond allegiance, beyond eternity.

"In the night of 'commentary,' or commentaire, *there shines—utter daring or fierce irony?—the proud verb* taire, *'to be silent,'" he said. "Any commentary must take off from what is silent in the text, what has knowingly or inadvertently been left unsaid."*

Comment? 'How?' O insistent question of all beginnings.

How can we be?

How can we follow?

How can we die?

You had to learn to deserve your truth. The Jews know that it is not enough to believe in a truth, that we must, each time, deserve it. There is no merit but in the stubborn effort to reach it. Does stating a truth mean you are sure of deserving it? Where could we find such certainty?

Ah, to grow into what we try to deserve.

What we do deserve—our share of a word—lies hidden, perhaps, between the lines of the book. No doubt, the strength of creation depends on not knowing this.

We can never know the value of the book. It can only be measured in terms of its resistance against the abyss. And who knows to what point the book can be lost?

Nomadism. Le Nom, 'the Name,' justifies the nomad. The Jew inherited the Name and, at the same time, lost his place on earth. The nomad takes on himself the unstated Name.

To drain all blood from the voice.
The voice is the straight way. It follows the tracks
of the letters. It is the book's blood.

You have no more voice. You have given your
blood. You have written.

The book's silence is sacrifice of the voice.

All writing is graven silence, mountaintops looming
on the far side of the voice.

Outside any constellation, it is the sparsile stars
which fascinate.)

"Just think," he said, "how many words a word can contain, and how they subtly undermine it.

"But do not look too closely. If you set a single one free, hundreds will attack you. Will the last one end up getting the better of you?"

Any word is a place open to attack by formidable words ready to usurp the book when nobody is watching.

"Isn't it strange," he said. "The word, which shatters the word in order to break free, for a moment holds the key to the book."

One letter in common is enough for two words to know each other.

The act of writing may be nothing but an act of controlled violence, the time it takes to move on to a new stage of violence. The book explodes with infuriating legibility.

All shattered writing has the form of a key.

O crumbled word, O book turned to dust. You thought you had done with letters, with symbols. But is that possible? Dust begets more dust.

It is clear that, facing nothingness, any sense is nonsense, any reality crushingly unreal, any alliance a sealed avowal of its useless strength.

Pages full of eyes turned towards death, towards evening.
Long have we searched the horizon in the dark.

O spent point, infinite defense of the book.
A single grain of sand holds out against the desert.

("In the word commentaire," *he repeated, "there are the words* taire, se taire, faire taire, *'to be silent, to fall silent, to silence,' which quotation demands.")*

All other life ceases in the life put into words.

The difference between the living and the dead is that the living talk while the dead do not.
Our body decays when it is suddenly robbed of its language, no longer conversant with itself, unable to form, to inform, to confirm.
We speak to the dead in order to bring them back to life. All we manage is the illusion of a general resurrection.
Light also is a word which begets other, explosive words.
Night, reign of respite after the explosion. Blind regrouping of our lights.

The Book of Resemblances
(1976)

"Resemblance with which, elsewhere, the questioning from one work to another reached its first—final—halt becomes an occasion for new and close inquiry, complementary, as we say of two colors. We do not yet know where it will lead, except that it has already taken us to the other bank of the same inexhaustible book," he said.

What is to be read will always remain to be read.

You read. You tie yourself to what comes untied—to what unties you within your ties.
You are a knot of correspondences.

. . . a knot of innocence, craftiness, of things likely and unlikely, of infinite faithfulness.

ED, OR THE FIRST MIST

Judaism is present wherever a human being is mistreated and persecuted. Yet the Jew is alone with his fate. The joys of his brothers he will share but for a moment. He always withdraws in order to exist, because distance is his best defense. Relations with him must be in terms of this withdrawal, this necessary distance where he moves, speaks and dies, as if his road engendered always more roads, as if only a roll of parchment could contain his law because, a concrete image of his wanderings, its endless unrolling could represent this incalculable distance punctuated by commandments, which the Jew must cover.

Language is a brew of resemblances—their test and countertest. Writing, then, means using any kind of likeness, marking its stages and degrees.

What we see in an image restores its significance for us, as if its reproduction in the mind were a solid passageway to the unveiled image, a bridge as well as a revelation of its meaning.

Inquiry occurs at this level of approach.

The universe is conspicuous for its likeness to the intimate universe in which we move, for its projection in our heart of hearts, where we no longer distinguish what is from what is only its avowed, accepted likeness.

> *(Resemblance sheds the unessential. It reenters essence into the circuit of forms, ideas, metaphors and connections—the preserved essential aspects of the relation and kinship of objects.*
>
> *"O Sarah," Yukel had written, "we were so alike that likeness never made any sense to us."*
> *Thus God, "El," has no likeness because He can only be like God.*

*"Can we be like Him, Who, in His essence, is with-
out likeness?" asked Reb Eliav.*

*He was told: "Are we not the image of the void
which has no image?"*

*Reb Lior, however, held a different opinion: "If
God, as we know, has chosen to manifest Himself in a
point, is it not to proclaim His likeness to a point?"*

*And he added: "Once we have stripped down to
being no more than a point in any book, our resemblance with God will be consummate."*

*"The point reveals God outside resemblance," Reb
Benchabat wrote elsewhere.)*

.

Nothing is true. Everything could be.

It is our misery that we cannot hold on to the whole life that was
ours, that we despair and want to die rather than admit defeat.

"Innumerable names nest in each single one.
"There will always be birds to fill the empty space with their
cries," he said.

"God is now victory of the wing, now the lethal instrument of its
defeat. The happy possibility of flight for the creature that resembles
Him, and the nail which pins it to the ground or wall: hope or misfortune.
"The mind knows only this double-faced God," he also said.

Shades of names, changing hue of clouds.
To name: to sort nuances of color.

Cloud in the diamond: bad portion of dark that so depreciates precious stones.

Yet in the southern sky, O Magellanic clouds, are you not matchless, double patch of light?

We count on blood resembling blood in our thirst for silence. Solitude under the skin.

.

Any book is but a dim likeness of the lost book.

"In each of us," he said, "there is a book that transforms us into words, as blood forms in the blood.

"To each utterance, each word, corresponds a heartbeat.

"The book's price is the price of an alliance."

Body present in its noises. The soul is a word swollen with remote blood.

There is no end, brother, to your ending up in the same word.

Our pen drinks deep at the veins of the moment.

(Procession of faces. Mad night of revelry. Likeness gambles its death, its likeness.

The curse that has, from the beginning, lain on all faces, on all revels that explode the face: this space of n dimensions.

"The divine prohibition is not against images, but against the likeness every image introduces. God wants no face-to-face," he said.

To recognize yourself in . . . To multiply your likenesses.

Fatal representation! As if in trying to be—to reveal myself—I only brought nothingness to light.

*We shall foil the common sight: we shall celebrate
fire, pupil burning within pupil.)*

In the beginning was the word that wanted to resemble.

Thus God confronted His likeness in the Word, and man his in
God.

All creation is an achievement of likeness, an act in which it takes
the risk of asserting itself.

What we create resembles us. Only across likeness—as across an
ocean—could God create man.

To say that God made us in His image only confirms this: a logical
deduction.

God fits perfectly into human logic, which is always short of in-
consistencies.

"Creation rejects us" means it ceases to resemble us, it questions
its likeness to us who had in vain tried to curb our resembling it.

It makes as little sense to declare that God will come where He
is expected as to declare that He will not come where He is not.

To have faith does not mean to expect God, but to make Him
expect us in order to quench our own desire of anticipation.

God is the illogical expectation of all expectation, its transfiguring
eternity.

God voices the expectation of voice.

Delight of desire where we only desire to live.

"The book is illogical absence of any existence in writing, a proof
of God," he said.

He also said: "What seems illogical often gives us providential
access to divine logic: a door where there is no door."

"To exist in the book could only mean absenting ourselves. God absents Himself in God," wrote Reb Saltiel.

No more logic once we face the unknown; instead, the absurd spectacle of logic overthrown, literally thrown all over the ground, a heap of broken levers.

Heavier than the world, the unknown. We cannot bear it.

"What strength could rival that of the void?" asked Reb Basri. "It is nothing and, all by itself, sustains All."

The unknown does not crush the void. It dazzles it.

Life has at its disposal all the colors it kindles; death, a single one which it imposes.

Writer and painter part company at the first ray of sun.

One color only for the word, that of death. One death only for the word, that of color. Death's color is forever: black ashes and white ashes mingling in water.

The writer banks on two colors and dies of one of them.

One color: enough to blind us.

Someday, white will stop being a color and be at last an abyss.

"Black will engulf us," he said.

The unknown stands at the end of life and at the beginning of death.

For the known, there is no way out except within the known. The unknown is a dead end, a horizon walled up.

Perhaps the exit is an answer; the dead end, a question.

The problem is not death, but the way out.

The way out: the hole you dig within your pale.

At the bottom of the known, where the mind surrenders, the un-known lies snug.

The void has the unknown for openers.

The book leans on the void.

God is the cry of a white word our letters trace for the eye.

The point of any pen is that of a cry.

God's cry is the cry of all absence.

"God has taken the idea of absence to its highest degree. At this altitude, the Book opens to the Book," wrote Reb Ségré.

God is absence of book; and the book, a slow deciphering of its absence.

No book outside God.

Intimations   The Desert
(1978)

INTIMATIONS

"Does day resemble night, and night, day, in mutual dependency, just as the word resembles silence, and the universe its absence, to the point of sameness: a day of night, a night of day?

"The instant adds its intimations to ours.

". . . intimations of voracious light at the edge of evening; dizzying chasm of dark in the purest noontime," wrote Reb Aboulbaka.

. . . this invisible crack that will one day destroy the wall.

"One bolt of lightning is enough to disfigure the sky. Then the infinite resembles a wounded man as God resembles us in the inflected emptiness of our death.

"O jeopardized circle!" Reb Hamoun had written.

Resemblance is the tragic—or comic—image of nothingness.

It is in unassignable death that we resemble one another.

"These intimations . . ."

"What do you suspect me of? I have come without ulterior motive. I wanted to see you again, chat a little . . ."

"I would like to believe you. And yet, your words . . ."

"Have I said something to offend you?"

"No, not really. But behind your words, those others, as if you were reading. Drawing them from a book, one might say."

"What words? What book?

"We have always been frank with each other. You know all about me. Have I ever betrayed you?"

"I begin to feel . . . In fact, I suspect . . ."

"What do you suspect? Explain."

". . . precisely this book whose pages fill with words as ours vanish into the air."

"What mysterious pages are you talking about? Are we writing? There is no paper on the table to abet us, no pen between our fingers."

"We are reading; this much is undeniable. All we need do is observe each other. Just follow my eyes the way I have followed yours from the moment you came into this room. We talk with the words our reading lacks.

"What we thought we said was hiding what we perhaps tried to express, but did not reveal."

"Are you insinuating that we have not talked at all?"

"Silence is inside the word as something to be read. A book is forever to be lost."

"Your book?"

"Perhaps the book erased so many times that only a mere inkling of it is left."

"The book of our silence, the desert."

"Yes, they are like sand, those soft, crumbly bits of eraser around our deleted words and in the end, O treacherous light or, rather, wound, the stubborn, mad hope of a possible bond, this perverse worm, this maggot in the sun."

(Every word mimics its likeness within the unlikeness where it is confined.

God died of wanting to be without likeness, of pushing likeness steeped in itself to unchallengeable perfection.

The scream tears through likeness.)

THE DESERT

"The word of our origin is a word of the desert, O desert of our words," wrote Reb Aslan.

"There is no place for the man whose steps head toward his place of birth;
"as if being born meant only walking toward your birth.
"My future, my origin," he said.

"There is no possible return if you have gone deep into the desert. Come from elsewhere, the elsewhere is your twin horizon.
"Sand, the asking. Sand, the reply. Our desert has no limits," wrote Reb Semama.

He held a bit of sand in each hand: "On the one hand, questions, on the other, answers. Same weight of dust," he also said.

To create means to make the future the past of all your actions.

With exemplary regularity the Jew chooses to set out for the desert, to go toward a renewed word that has become his origin.

"In creating, you create the origin that swallows you," wrote Reb Sanua.

"The origin is an abyss."

Reb Behit.

·

"If God spoke in the desert it was to deprive His word of roots, so that the creature should be His privileged bond. We shall make our souls into a hidden oasis," said Reb Abravanel.

"And of His written word?" asked his disciple, "what shall we make of that?"

"Of his fiery vocables we shall make a book of inconsumable fire," replied Ren Abravanel.

But Reb Hassoud, whose bold statements and commentaries were most often badly received by the interpreters, spoke up:

"A wandering word is the word of God. It has for echo the word of a wandering people. No oasis for it, no shadow, no peace. Only the immense, thirsty desert, only the book of this thirst, the devastating fire of this fire reducing all books to ashes at the threshold of the obsessive, illegible Book bequeathed us."

"What have we done other than forever call ourselves into question by examining everything down to the buzzing fly? Here is our humble merit and the source of our despair," wrote Reb Feroush.

"At which moment of painful impotence must we impose on the book an end to our reading?

"I close my eyes. I refuse to go on.

"Let the book come finally free of our chains," he had noted.

The Ineffaceable   The Unperceived
(1980)

Inexhaustible last book, ineffaceable, come before all others, perceived by none, like the light pushing the dark from its field, like dark never curtailed by the light . . .

You perceive what dies with you. What lasts cannot be grasped.

THE PRE-EXISTENCE OF THE
LAST BOOK

The last book is the book of God, a book which would have been man's first had he been able to write it.

Then there would be books and books all claiming to be the last.

We shall never know the last book; perhaps because we have always, dimly, known it?
Likewise God.

You do not write what you know, but what you are unaware you know and then discover, without surprise, you have always known.
As one knows that death is the end or that in a few hours it will be day.
As if you were, in short, exploring a past diverted from the course of your memory, but originally yours.

Munificent memory! Oblivion, too, is a pledge of the future.

Impassive permanence of the past; unexplored lining of days to come.

"A poet finds; a scholar rediscovers.
"All discovery is but patient conquest of oblivion," said Reb Rafat.

Oblivion is the nearest landmark. Thus the future sets limits for the creator in order to renew and perpetuate creation.

Discoveries still to be made give way under the weight of all that may never come to be known.

"If eternity lies behind us it is because the future is but a dreaded or expected past revealed by the moment.

"Then any achievement would only be self-recognition," he had written.

Intuition is a thin veil that gradually yields to the force of desire.

Ah, to keep our eyes closed jealously. All of knowledge lies behind our pupils.

"To see means to connect the thing seen with a knowledge that enriches ours," Reb Zalal had noted.

And Reb Hayat: "No discovery but has issued from the arbitrary idea we had of it.

"This idea was the right approach, the beginning of discovery."

"Resemblance of what is already created and what is soon to be.

"The book comes before. God comes before. The universe comes before. The creature comes before. Every morning teaches us so," wrote Reb Lamza.

God's wager is a wager of likeness.

To push likeness to the point of unlikeness that would define our likenesses.

"Whom do I resemble?" is perhaps the basic question man asks of God as well as of his prosaic brothers.

"In each of us there is an enemy of God's whose rash ambition gravely troubles our mind," Reb Maad had written.

"It is through the mind God holds us in bondage," said Reb Ezri.

And Reb Asson: "The thought of God pulls our thinking to such heights that it has no strength left for thinking.

"To escape God would mean to clip the wings of thought and make it hang on to our coattails."

"Could it be that God's thinking is but an impudence of Thought, a haughty disdain of barriers that, like an imperious un-thought, challenges our thinking caught in its own threads like a spider in its net?

"More than our heart God rules our mind," Reb Bahour will write in turn.

And was it not Reb Ragay who wrote: "Our sky is our soil. We think, eyes turned toward the ground"?

And Reb Galab: "Thought—luminous silkworm— is the larva of a butterfly. Master of the universe it is locked into. The cruel duty of the thinker is to choke it in the chrysalis before it breaks out, trusting to its suicidal flight."

"It is the worm produces riches, never the butterfly," Reb Labod liked to repeat.

"Limits create limits," Reb Baadi had noted. "The abyss is perhaps the failure of all creation."

God succumbs to His own arrows. Revenge of the target!

2

(*"The practice of the book is a promise of renewal. The universe is transformed from reading to reading, so that you read only what was waiting to be read,"* wrote Reb Lashem.

And Reb Mekhaalim: "What cannot be changed is not eternal, but dead.")

3

And he said:

"In the inevitable hour of dismissal, when the echo already echoes sheer nothing, I must take leave of my brothers.

"Those who knew me will say: He came with the book and with the book he disappeared.

"Those who did not know me will say: The image we retain of his work is now a cradle, now a grave.

"They will be both wrong and right, for I follow the book in its progressive mastery over the abyss and in its headlong fall."

And Reb Assin said:

"God is the consenting victim of the Book."

"O death, distinctly legible in every word."

4

(They looked all over the cemetery for the stranger's grave.

They were told he had not wanted to be buried, but had donated his body to Science.

So they each opened the book of his they held dearest.

One put in a blossom of water dropped from his eyes; another, a pebble picked up on the road.

They were nameless warrants of the trace.

Had Reb Doubbah not written: "The trace of our passage on earth, the mark made by our works: invisible. It lies buried in the soul of a few people like us. Up to them to reveal it on occasion.

"To how many unknown friends do we owe our portion of permanence?"

And he had added for Reb Samhob, his revered teacher, who, in order to be forgotten, had under an assumed name taken refuge in a village at the edge of the desert, where nobody would have dreamed to look for him: "Do not worry about your trace. You are the only one who cannot erase it.")

The Little Book of Subversion
Above Suspicion
(1982)

Subversion is the very movement of writing: the very movement of death.

The written page is no mirror. Writing means confronting an unknown face.

Driven mad, the sea, unable to die of one single wave.

THE QUESTION OF SUBVERSION

("We threaten what threatens us. Subversion is never one-way," he had noted.

Through its title and the book which already contains it, this little book hooks onto the ten volumes of the Book of Questions. *This also is no doubt subversion.*

If I give the same title to two different texts, are they not all the more opposites for the arbitrary, circumstantial unity imposed on them?
The conflict is internal.

Thus the word that names us is the same that will sooner or later violate the ineffable Name of God,
because no creature can bear the absence of the divine name.
Had he not written: "Through His Name, God is at the mercy of man?"
The revolt of a shadow hastens the coming of light, just as illegibility, at war with itself, prepares us for perfect legibility.

We need continuity, resemblance, reciprocity as we need fresh bread.

Man is his own origin as well as his own beyond.

It takes only a smile to stop a tear. It takes only a tear to shatter a smile for good.

"The subversive is not necessarily what proclaims itself as such from the start. On the contrary, it often

is what, to act more surely on the beings and things it opposes, sides with them unreservedly to the point of speaking in their name.

"In this way white can topple white into a fatal abyss of whiteness by claiming to be whiteness itself," *he said.*

Nothingness remains the unconscious stake of subversion.)

"I have only bad disciples," said a sage. "When they try to copy me, they betray me; when they believe they resemble me, they discredit themselves."

"I am luckier than you," replied another sage. "Having spent my life questioning, I of course have no disciples at all."

And he added: "Is this not the reason I was sentenced for subversive activities by the Council of Elders?"

"A knot cannot make another knot, but any thread can.

"Hence every knot is unique.

"It is the same with our relation to God, to mankind, to the world," he said.

Thought has no strings attached: it lives by encounters and dies of solitude.

"Look at me," he said, "listen. I am the perpetual questioning that revives the well.

"It is the well you see and hear. In the hour of thirst you will bend down to drink."

To every book its twenty-six letters, to every letter its thousands of books.

Trembling, he handed his teacher a notebook filled with words in his hand: his book.

"Why are you trembling?" asked the teacher.

"These pages," he answered, "burn my fingers like sheets of ice. I'm trembling with cold."

"Tell me what is in these pages," the teacher continued.

"I do not know," he replied.

"If you do not know, who will?" said the teacher.

"The book knows."

NOTEBOOK

The sky wins out over the book, but not over the sand, which curdles it in every grain.

Only the weight of silence can be thought here.

God did not carve His word into stone, but into an eternal moment of petrified silence.

The breaking of the Tablets is above all the fundamental act that allowed divine writing to pass from silence into the silence ratified by all writing.

Richness of utter poverty.

"Writing," he said, "is an act of silence directed against silence, the first positive act of death against death."

> ("Beyond what I might still have to say.
> "Your portion to read. Mine, to disappear.
> "Intruder," he had noted.
>
> "It is the sky descends onto the earth, not the earth rising up into the sky. Our planet does not, alas, have the lightness of blue or of shadow," he said.
> And added: "Thus death will descend on our stiffened bodies.")

The written is binding. Perhaps we write only to *detach* ourselves without realizing that this detachment is a manner of respecting our attachments to the last,

. . . to the last, that is, to the point where the attachment we have honored appears to us in the form of a new one.

.

We read—as we cut grass—what the night will take from us.

Thought needs to stoop to conquer new heights. Its peaks are also its limits.

This is why we might say the unthought is thought that *cannot be made to stoop*.

We are the prey of various scriptures.

"If truth existed," he said, "it would be our only enemy.
"Luckily it does not exist, so we are free to invent enemies."

"I have studded the night with demands," he also said. "Some have wanted to take them for stars in love with their glitter."

All of time has room in one look.
The infinite opens our eyes, the instant closes them.
No eternity but in oblivion.

He said: "Generous and merciless word. Everything was either granted or denied me by you, including the moment now swelling my heart with love and that other one that will soon make it beat so feebly only death on the alert will hear it."

Any reading sets limits. An unlimited text yields a new reading every time, a reading it partly escapes.
What always remains to be read is its one chance of survival.

To live without asking "Why" means dodging the question "How to die," means accepting a death without origin.

The history of thought is perhaps only the daring thought of history lived at the level of thought—like a branch cut back to the trunk.

An endless book can find completion only in that of its unforeseeable prolongations.

The air you breathe forces you to give it back to the air.
This is the nature of breath.
Your chest is too narrow for the heavenly gift.

"I am no doubt the memory of my books. But to what point have my books been my memory?" he asked.

Thought is not born in light. It is light.
Would I, for my part, say it is born to the night?

"I love," he also said, "those fleeting thoughts caught between the haze of sleep and the timid glimmer of day,
"between the already less dark nothing where they were sunk and the flowering grass surprised by the first look."

How is thought defined?—Not by what it is, but by what it closes in on.
Then what we call thought is perhaps only its capacity to encircle what is offered.
So we never know how far its curiosity will take us, while it, to match our faith in language, also subordinates thinking to the unforeseeable success of its formulation.

A ciliate, winged, tufted grain: thought.

He compared thought now to a wheat field, now to an ocean. He was twice wrong. Thought has the charge of a grain and the dimensions of an ocean.

Bastard thought, poor well.

Thought running to seed. The unthought has no stem.

.

"The unthought," he said, "is the beyond of the book, its inner horizon."

If I try to define the unthought by comparing it to a certain ferment, it immediately seems, rather, the infinite torment of my thinking.

So the beyond of the book is still the book.

I cannot think the unthought except by starting from the limit. The region I head for is uncharted.

Any step belongs to thought.
To the unthought: sudden lack of rungs.

To know every interval of the infinite, like the layout of a house. The moment is a minuscule door to duration. We enter, once again tiny.

In my house, time finds no shelter.

"I can say without risk of error," he had noted, "that the unthought is nothing but the feared crumbling of the bridge between two hazy shores."

The earth turns in the bold thought of its roundness and in the unthought void that supports it.

What has the power to undo cannot itself be undone.

We always write along a thread of Nothing.

To say of thought, as of a fruit, that it has set.

No issue but into the unknown.

The man who leaves—like Abram—where does he go? Sets out in search of his identity and discovers *the other*. He knows from the start he will perish of this *otherness* in the unfathomable distance that separates him from himself, out of which rises the face of his solitude.

We live on this side. We die, always, on the other; but the line is in the mind.

THE LITTLE BOOK OF SUBVERSION ABOVE SUSPICION 187

Can we think otherness? We can only draw on our idea of it.

Could it be that our relation to the other is but the relation of two barren thoughts set heel to heel, where the unthought does not yet dare flaunt its triumph?

Likewise day and night turn their backs on each other, only to perish by their own weapons.

Aging wounds us. All our setbacks are bloody. But sometimes, at the lowest point of the curve, a spark of love is enough to brighten our night.

Never consider acquisitions as anything but a manifest irony of Nothing.

Having possessions means in a certain way living on the salutary humor of emptiness.

"The thinker is a seasoned fisherman," he said. "From the sea of the unthought he draws luminous thoughts—moonfish or globefish, pilotfish or flatfish—which, having swallowed the bait, wriggle for a moment between the blue of the sky and the blue of the sea before they stiffen, strangers, on the ground."

Terrifying couple: life atremble, death in stitches.

Thought is to life as the unthought to death: one and the same buoy.

For living as for dying, we will have used the same bobbin.

As a bedlamp lights only the space between bed and wall, freedom illumines but the shadow of one step.

It seems absurd, at first sight, to ask questions of absence.
Yet all our questions are really addressed to it.

"We rush so blindly toward the vast realms of absence that I am frightened.

"All becoming is but absence gradually assimilated," he said.

And added: "My soul has had its best part amputated, as a healthy body may lose its right arm.

"Ah, how it hurts me, physically, this missing part of myself.
"What can I conclude but that absence is revealed in pain."

Blood reddens the ink without, for all that, warming it.
Every word dies of exposure.

Our absence from the world is perhaps nothing but our presence
in the void.

You can count only the days you lose.

A glance whose solitude we could never imagine: the glance of
the Void.

Hide your wounds from the man who bears you ill will: they
would excite him.

"What is frightening you?"
"What settles down in your name and needs no justification."
"I do not follow."
"And what if I told you your truth is murderous?"

The Book of Dialogue
(1984)

THE SPOILS OF SPACE

"Is dialogue possible?"

"As life and death are."

"I live and I shall die."

"You live the impossibility of living which death has made possible so as to be able to bring it to an end."

"Where there is no beginning there can be no end."

"Every word is born of a word's ebb. We speak in tow to the tide."

.

("What does he say?"

"He says once life stops questioning death, and death, questioning life, there is no more hope. There is oblivion, the hell of oblivion."

"Or peace?"

"A hell of peace. Leaves on live coals."

"Ah, hold on to your book. It will protect you."

"Go on. Don't stop talking."

"I read our book over your shoulder. Ah, do not turn from what is written. You are both pen and hand."

"To read is to burn. Our only good."

"As long as you can decipher the book it will last.")

.

He said: "This blaze is perhaps just a book on fire between sky and ruins.

"A dialogue of quick flames and flames dying down."

And he added: "Stately oak whose branches no

longer form lines and whose leaves have stopped being words.

"Tree and book are banners of one and the same conflagration."

"Where is the fire?" he asked.

"Elsewhere, far off. You cannot see it from here except for the lambent light."

.

The writer burns for the book: his way of sparing it.

When the question was raised: "Is there such a thing as dialogue, and how can it come about between two strangers?" he replied: "There is *pre-dialogue*, our slow or feverish preparation for dialogue. Without any idea of how it will proceed, which form it will take, without being able to explain it, we are convinced in advance that the dialogue has already begun: a silent dialogue with an absent partner.

"Then afterward, there is *post-dialogue* or after-silence. For what we managed to say to the other in our exchange of words—or, rather, in our apprenticeship of words—says virtually nothing but this silence, silence on which we are thrown back by any unfathomable, self-centered word whose depth we vainly tried to sound.

"Then finally there is what could have been the actual dialogue, vital, irreplaceable, but which, alas, does not take place: it begins the very moment we take leave of one another and return to our solitudes."

Like dialogue, the book is approached in stages.

Then writing means climbing the steps of our lack.

At the peak, the Word.

("My life in the book is untenable," he had written, "yet, fool that I am, I hold on to this life.
"Help me. Share my words and my place.")

PRE-DIALOGUE, II

. . . this insignificant interval between death and dying.

One cannot accept or refuse, O death, emptiness, air, sun.

The "I" is the miracle of the "You."

"This follows from a certain logic," he said: "the 'I' to designate the 'You,' the 'You' to justify the 'I,' and 'He' for disappearing."

There is no present. There is a past haunted by the future and a future tormented by the past.
The present is the time of writing, both obsessed with and cut off from an out-of-time brimming with life.

> *(Now that all is silent within me, will I, who have hardly known how to talk to myself, still be able to speak? I almost cannot hear myself any more. On this 'almost' I shall rest my words or, rather, what stubbornly still wants to be words—though they be deaf to the call of the world—and take entire charge of them. Expressing nothing, they will express me all the better.)*

For pain, forgetting is an island of flowers.
Sweet smell of emptiness.

Fabulous a wing
unfolding in the paltry field of things.

Night finds no consolation in night, but in the lavish star bespangled with all its lights.

Others: a fiction.

THE DREAM

I have developed a habit; every morning, before going to my desk, say—in any case, before attending to any business—I sit for a moment in the armchair in one corner of the room, which is my refuge. My chair, since I have long adopted it.

This particular day at the usual hour, I tried, eyes half closed, to empty my mind and give free rein to the various thoughts assailing me, to be led by them without any precise aim, meaning neither to obey nor to bristle.

I was still waiting for my reflections and meditations to take off when I heard a knock at the door—I always take the precaution of closing it so that I will not be needlessly bothered—and, almost at the same moment, saw a young woman enter. I did not dare speak at first, paralyzed by her airy manner and the silence she imposed. A silence more exacting than that of the room.

She sat down in the matching armchair opposite mine, watched me for a brief moment, then asked me point-blank to be so kind as to tell her her name—but with so blighted a smile, such painfully insistent eyes that I trembled.

She must have realized that I was upset because she immediately got up again, embarrassed, it seemed, went toward the door—which she had left ajar on coming in—and, without paying me any more heed, disappeared.

Of this woman, of whom I know only that she one morning burst into my room only to vanish as suddenly, but whose strange request harries my memory, of this woman nothing much will be said in this book. Not of her infinitely sweet voice, nor even of the incurable wound she had come to pit against mine.

But her face and voice are only the more present in these pages. Her face, to feed my imagination, her voice, irrefutable proof that she is real.

Image of the book, voice that goes through it from one end to the other. Dew for an uncharted desert and dream of oases choked with sand.

ON THE THRESHOLD OF DIALOGUE

"What happens when we throw a ball against a wall? The wall bounces it back. But the way we pick it up and throw it again can vary according to the rules of the game.

"We go from ease to strain, slack off after exertion, all without forethought.

"Dialogue is the same way," he said.

The heart of dialogue beats with questions.

There are two silences within each silence, as there are two words within each word.

Speak up. Break down the wall.

The word of truth blossoms behind walls. Must we, ah, must we cleave stone to gather it?

"Chasms," he assured us, "communicate with each other through the spell they cast on us.

"Thus we are at the origin of their vertiginous appeal."

"But what is origin," he was answered, "except the vertigo of a hypothetical beginning?"

The abyss is the emptiness essential to the blossoming of universal memory.

This emptiness of the soul wraps us in darkness, O grotesque pillow from which we lift a face bathed in sweat.

Necessary nothingness.

.

"I have come to ask you some questions," said the disciple.

"Do not expect any lesson from me," replied the master. "We

have both received our share of the same light: our humble knowledge."

"Must I then leave you already?" said the disciple.

"Be patient. I shall do my best to help you. I shall teach you, by
and by, to unlearn. Such is the virtue of dialogue," replied the master.

Truth would lay claim to completion if incompletion did not war-
rant the failure of any truth that reaches its end.

.

He was crazy. He asked: "Is there a limit to the questions of the
book? Ah, where is this limit? Where is it pitched?"

He was wise. He replied: "The limit of day is the day."

A chance to endure? The book grants it only to the book. Sometimes, though, the author benefits.

He said: "If you go into the desert, silence no longer envelops
you. You become yourself such silence as makes the desert *speak*.

"Do you know what freedom is?" he also asked. "A long thread
we mean to cut, but which always escapes the scissors, so flawless
its transparency."

Truth is not tied to freedom. But there is no freedom that is not
a reading of truth.

He was crazy. He asked: "What can strike roots in the open?"

He was wise. He answered: "Perhaps the *unrootable*, at the precise moment of surprise."

There is a listening to death from which we cannot draw profit or
effect except in death.

"Death," he said, "is perhaps the deserted dead end at the turn
of a lively street, reverberating with echoes of interrupted dialogue."

Blossoming of the book. Dialogue is an afterbloom.

What seems just now to be taking shape has often already formed out of sight. The future periodically revises its contours.

.

A young man went to see his Teacher and said: "May I talk to you?"

The Teacher answered: "Come back tomorrow. Then we'll talk."

The day after, the young man came back and said: "May I talk to you?"

As on the day before, the Teacher answered: "Come back tomorrow. Then we'll talk."

"I came yesterday and asked you this same question," replied the young man, disappointed. "Do you refuse to talk to me?"

"We have been in dialogue since yesterday," replied the Teacher, smiling. "Whose fault if we have bad ears?"

(The event will never take place. It is the tenant of this "place never taken.")

The Journey
(1985)

To make the origin gain ground: vocation of all origin.

Truth can be told. It is the story of a life.
Everyone his truth, his untold tale.

When written, death is not death. It is unanimous life: *what gathers and what disperses.*
From one abyss to the next our journey remains that of the book. From a death without certainty to certain death.

Only the void answers the void; God's only reference is God.

THE LINE OF THE HORIZON

Death cultivates visibility.

There is no silent image.
There is a silence we lock it in.

Attracted by all of them, we can scrutinize only one image at a time.

For all the words of the language, we accompany only one word into death.

Our image of the cold is our own image out in the cold: anonymous sketch of a body shivering.

The image does not reflect reality, but, rather, shows the spectacular end of all reality.

To see, means to die; to watch, dying.

Wind and sand revel in worsting the eye, making it cry.

Yellowed with age, the image yields only nostalgia: image of a lost image.

The void is not invisible. There might be an image to suit it, be it that of its invisibility.

It is the impertinent non-representation of Nothingness.

They were ten around a table.
The discussion was getting heated.
Only one of the guests said nothing.
Distracted? Bored? On the contrary. He was listening with the

keenest attention for what, behind the deafening flood of words, re-
mained obstinately silent.

The oldest among them said to him: "Your attitude has given us
a true image of God. Like Him, you have tried to hear what we shall
never be able to express."

With book after book, with all my writing, have I questioned only
Judaism?

I think I discovered that Jewish writing in its relation to eternity
can only have issued from the ferocious combat of the book and its
image: the word of the image against the image of the word. Jewish
writing attests that the end of this fight is nowhere in sight.

Blank, the first and last page of the book.

Is the unpronounceable name, after standing for God's absence—
His all-presence—also the name of the book and, through the me-
diation of words, that of the writer and the Jew?

Translucent words, "writer," "Jew." They are nothing but the
sheer transparency of the word inside which they flounder in vain.

The ungraspable—the invisible—sometimes upsets us beyond
what we can bear.

God's disappearance confirms death's supremacy over life.
With God absent, there is no more eternity.
All light is added darkness.
The brush, without resources.

Not give to see, but see what is given.
To give up painting. To paint this giving up.

Far, far off, at the confines of oceans covered with foam, there
drifts our face, unrecognizable.

. . . but Judaism is life, is unshakable faith in life and in man.

THE BOOK READ, HERE
BEGINS THE READING OF THE BOOK

Say no to Nothingness. On this sentence I wanted to build the book, for what is living but saying no to Nothingness.

Nothing, obsession of God; Nothing, terror of the universe betrayed in a myriad eyes turned stars; Nothing, enemy of mankind; Nothing, finally, rival of the book.

A seemingly optimistic sentence referring us to the All, God, the Totality of totalities, the universe, man and the book, urging a separate approach to each inaccessible Totality.

But is All not already Nothing?

To live on Nothing, the shared life of the All.

To die at the foot of the All, of the brief Survival of Nothing.

We shall have followed the path cleared by Jewish words. Two sentences have accompanied our wanderings. For breathing in: *"God created man in His image"*; for breathing out: ". . . . *dust thou art and to dust thou shalt return."*

Invincible like a wave, an ocean, the tenacious past rises and ever riles the future.

The Jew will be saved by the book he has himself helped preserve.

Every book is perhaps the renewed tale of this rescue.

What if the face of God were an abuse of faces—an abusive face supplanting ours?

What if it were not God who had modeled man in His likeness, but man who one day took to imagining God in his image?

Pride and humility of the creature also able to create.

And what if divine Creation in its incompletion were founded solely on the despair that all creation plunges us into?

What if the book with all its wiles and daring were only mad resistance against the emptiness of the last page?

In Place of an Afterword

LETTER FROM SARAH TO YUKEL

I am going to die, Yukel, it must be, in this book we do not have time to finish writing.

I am dying within myself for this unfinished book.

How many untouched pages before us!

Yet are they without wrinkles, as empty as we think?

It is as if a shadow lay on them, deep inside and on their calm surface, shadow of an unhappy hand so heavy, so cold it seems lifeless at the edge of the table.

How heavy this hand at one extreme of my body! How heavy this heart in the moist hollow of my hand!

The book could have been ours. I thought it would be. I hoped so. This was clearly madness. What life could appropriate the book all for itself? Death could, perhaps. Then all these still untried pages would yield to the accrued number of words that nobody could read within time.

A book for no one, at the end of a love without frontiers.

Tomorrow is another moment of the book to be deciphered.

LETTER FROM YUKEL TO SARAH

This book stripped of words, Sarah, nevertheless contains our story because it is a book written by death, and we have been dead from the moment we lost our name.

A thick blanket of snow covers our words. They are so distant, so forgotten by our brothers that they are perhaps no longer even words spoken by humans, but distorted echoes of our buried screams.

The absence of the book consecrates our absence. Like me, you are alive only where we no longer are, that is, where all mirrors lie shattered at the foot of a single one, behind which we stand, immobile.

The void we are examining is not that of the book we are quietly plunging into. It is the void of their book, Sarah, of which we are a transparent page, hostile against any resurgence of symbols, any belated flowering.

Out of the silence of centuries, discrete words will, one day, surface for us and then for those who have gradually learned to read us in the void. Our book is for tomorrow.

> *(Does the book, here, take the place of love? The book is an object of love. Love manifests itself in the book by hugging, stroking, biting sentences, words, letters and, outside the book, by an unveiled passion for the wounds become writing, fertile lesions whose lips we spread open like a vulva to allow the sperm of death in.*
>
> *"Your parts, woman, are the white abyss of the book which once bled for an unheard-of word the flood of our words has since carried away," he said.*
>
> *But hate and love are also in the book: hate and envy of God quickened by an undeciphered text, a text under the text, for which the latter exhausts and consumes itself.*

There is fire in the page to kindle and snuff its whiteness, eternal morning of the first, the only, book.)

From the terrace of my hotel I watch how countless birds—the waves—die with spread wings on the water.

And I say to myself, this must be the way books die, given that they begin with words taking wing toward the sky.

At times, one makes a powerful effort to rise into the air, but immediately falls back, cutting a hole in the sea.

Our graves are not those of words, nor those of fish or seabirds, graves eternally moving. They disdain and disturb the order of time.

"There is no end to the sea or the book," you said. "Words unwind the transparent thread of days in the continual back-and-forth of their life and death left to themselves.

"Though the pen grow weaker and weaker, the book nevertheless continues writing, in white letters, to the end."

Making a book could mean exchanging the *void of writing* for *writing the void.*

(Nothing is alike any more. Remains what is to be remembered, that is, what is still standing between what was and what is no more: simulacrum of object, of language, of light.

Writing is the dawning solitude of the letter.)

UNIVERSITY PRESS OF NEW ENGLAND publishes books under its own imprint and is the publisher for Brandeis University Press, Brown University Press, Clark University Press, University of Connecticut, Dartmouth College, Middlebury College Press, University of New Hampshire, University of Rhode Island, Tufts University, University of Vermont, and Wesleyan University Press.

ABOUT THE AUTHOR

Edmond Jabès died in Paris in 1991 at the age of 78. He settled in France with his wife, Arlette, and two daughters after being expelled from his native Egypt with other Jews during the 1956 Suez Crisis. He was regarded as one of France's most important contemporary writers. His awards include the Prix des Critiques (1970), the Prize for Arts, Letters and Science of the Foundation of French Judaism (1982), the Grand Prix National de Poésie (1987), and the Italian Pasolini and Cittadella prizes (1983 and 1987). His other works available in English from Wesleyan University Press are *The Book of Dialogue* (1987), *The Book of Resemblances* in three volumes, and *The Book of Questions* issued in two volumes in 1991.

ABOUT THE TRANSLATOR

Rosmarie Waldrop was born in Germany and educated at the universities of Freiburg, Aix-Marseilles, and Michigan. She has translated from French and German and is the author of numerous creative and critical works. Her most recent books of poetry are *Peculiar Motions* (1990) and *The Reproduction of Profiles* (1987). She has also written two novels, *A Form / of Taking / It All* (1990) and *The Hanky of Pippin's Daughter* (1987). Her translations of Jabès won a Columbia University Translation Center Award in 1978. She lives in Providence, Rhode Island.

Library of Congress Cataloging-in-Publication Data

Jabès, Edmond.
  [Poems. English. Selections]
From the book to the book : an Edmond Jabès reader / translated from the French by Rosmarie Waldrop, with additional translations by Pierre Joris, Anthony Rudolf, and Keith Waldrop.
  p.   cm.
ISBN 0–8195–5242–9. — ISBN 0–8195–6252–1 (pbk.)
  1. Jabès, Edmond—Translations into English.   I. Title.
PQ2619.A112A28   1991
841'.914—dc20

91–50368